CHARLIEZZ...

Trupthi Guttal
and
Zeeshan Farooqui

First published in India 2011 by Frog Books
An imprint of Leadstart Publishing Pvt Ltd
1 Level, Trade Centre
Bandra Kurla Complex
Bandra (East) Mumbai 400 051 India
Telephone: +91-22-40700804
Fax: +91-22-40700800
Email: info@leadstartcorp.com
www.leadstartcorp.com / www.frogbooks.net

Marketing Office:
Unit: 122 / Building B/2
First Floor, Near Wadala RTO
Wadala (East) Mumbai 400 037 India
Phone: +91-22-24046887

US Office:
Axis Corp, 7845 E Oakbrook Circle
Madison, WI 53717 USA

ISBN 978-93-81576-55-7

Publisher and Managing Editor: Swarup Nanda
Books Editor: Sharmila Ramnani
Design Editor: Mishta Roy

Typeset in Book Antiqua
Printed at Repro India Ltd, Mumbai

Price — India: Rs 150; Elsewhere: US $6

Dedication

*To our grand parents and our dear friends
whom we cherish whole heartedly.*

About the authors

Trupthi Guttal born and brought up in Bangalore. She has graduated from M.S.Ramaiah College of engineering, Bangalore, but hailing from a rich cultural belt of North Karnataka is a 24 year old budding author. Having pursued Engineering in the field of Chemical, she is currently working in a design consultancy firm as a Design Engineer.

She can be contacted at trupthichem@gmail.com

Zeeshan Farooqui born and brought up in Dharwad. He has graduated from KLE's college of Engineering, Belgaum. He is a Chemical Engineer by profession. He is presently working as Assistant Manager in a design consultancy firm in Bangalore. He has completed his MBA from IBMT, Bangalore, in marketing management.

He can be contacted at zeestar@rediffmail.com

Contents

PREAMBLE

"Great! He called again," I said in my typical irritated tone to Zahir. He smiled and said a word or two, to support me. Then I forcibly, rather we forcibly, dragged ourselves to meet the person who kills by words and looks! (Term still not found in the dictionary).

We took a bunch of sheets and books and files and big files and, most importantly, our brains (temporarily supported by a man-made easy device – the calculator!) and marched to meet the 'CEO'.

We entered the room meekly and took our seats. "Hmmmmm… What is this enquiry about?" started our CEO. We thought, 'Oh there he starts off with a bouncer and hell, he will not rest in peace till he bowls us all out for 0!' Finally after three hours of a not-so-friendly match, we walked out of the ground to our dugout.

"Not bad, he didn't kill or shoot us," I said with a giggle. A roar of laughter could be heard from our team.

"He is conked off, the old-guy," said Vicky with a big grin on his face. We agreed in unison that it was the result of our 'bad karma'.

Before you readers wonder what's this fuss about, I will

give you the starters. This is a design company (name not mentioned for the fear of... let us put it straight for the fear of being in a pool of the unemployed lot). We are the three monkeys working under a believer of 'HIMSA' CEO! This is a kind of job that every Chemical Engineer aspires. The hard core chemical engineering stuff (I mention stuff to spare you all from the details).

I dedicate this book to our team who, as a team, fought against the grey cell discriminating 'walking encyclopaedia', our CEO, the honourable Dr. Rao!

So now I will give you a sneak preview of our lives in the subsequent chapters. Hope you all enjoy and stay with me till the last ink mark in this book.

CHAPTER 1
GRAND MASSACRE

"What is specific humidity?" quipped the 'blast furnace' (another name for our dear CEO).

While I fumbled hopelessly to utter those golden words, Zahir shot the answer to cool the old chap.

"Hmmm, okay, you guys know something! Check up with the marketing team if this enquiry can be quoted." We came out of the room relieved that it didn't take our 'precious time'.

Doctor' as we addressed him, is an adorable 76-year-old Britannica, the company CEO, and he gives more than what normally is expected from a person of his age. He is the pillar of the company.

But alas, as is the case with typical old people, the tempers are always a problem to manage. Working with him, we realized that if we can handle this guy, then the world is in our hands!

Oops, the phone is ringing. I crossed my fingers half hoping it was not 'blast furnace' again.

Damn! It was him and, as usual, going alone to him is like luring a hungry lion. I forgot to tell you the rule of this department; it goes like this – 'God Almighty, in case the 'blast furnace' calls us, under no circumstances should we go alone and we should be accompanied by the 'ring master', (who will show a whip to scare the lion)'. So in our department, Zahir was the ring master as he could handle the old guy pretty well. However, there were some cases wherein the lion had devoured the ring master, but since we had no other hopes, we relied on him.

So I, Vikram (Vicky) and the ring master set off to meet Doctor, not knowing what the future held for us.

I didn't mention about the third monkey in our group, Vicky (Vikram Pundit). I can describe him as silent, timid natured and the most hard working amongst the three of us.

He usually came on time, worked or rather slogged throughout the day and spent most of his time doing R & D (Research and Development).

"Zahir, in this document it is mentioned as..." This is how Vicky would sound at any time of the day.

Zahir was a good natured, reserved, bit boring kind of a guy who was bogged down by tedious work. So most of the time, he was either busy or pretended to be busy. He would generally stay away and be aloof from the crowd keeping to himself. In his world, only one thing mattered - work. He headed the process department comprising of two engineers - Khushi Patil and Vikram Pundit (Vicky).

Work-wise, we three shared a great rapport and, as I mentioned earlier, we believed in sharing our work. So if anyone had to meet the 'furnace' all the three of us went to him. At least two witnesses are required when a murder occurs, you see.

We went to his room, sat obediently as Gandhiji's three monkeys.

"Hmmmmm… so what is this project about?" he asked.

Both Vicky and I looked at the ring master to make the first move.

"Sir, this is an enquiry for a gas cooler; here we have to cool the gas using water as a cooling medium," said the ring master confidently.

"Hmmmmm … so have you people gone through the details?" asked the furnace.

We again looked at the ring master who he said, "Ah... Um... Yeas sir."

"So, what do they want?"

"Actually sir, they have asked us to cool the gas using water as the cooling medium," muttered the ring master half hoping we make our moves. But no! We sat still looking at both of them.

"Oh really, is that what is mentioned in this document?" Doctor asked, this time sternly indicating we were not answering him.

"Ah... ah... actually sir, I am handling this project," Vicky said meekly squinting his eyes.

"Then why the hell are you not talking? Have you read this document or not?"

"Sir, well... I... yeah... have read... but not completely... there are a hundred pages... so it is not complete…"

"What do you mean 'not complete'? Bloody, you had two days' time! What were you doing? *Bhajan*?" thundered Doctor.

By this time all three of us knew what was going to happen next; as expected we had a mouthful.

"Do you people have some seriousness in your jobs? Have you done your engineering? I don't know why I have such Charlies like you in my office. How many times have I told you to read this? Can you tell me what we had done in the previous project for a similar type of job?"

This time I had to talk because he was looking straight at me.

"*Haan*… sir… previous job… we had… ah... taken gas to cool the water… oh sorry I mean … we had water as the cooling media to cool the gas."

"Oh brilliant, I didn't know we had done this before! What is this madam? Are you fooling around? All the three of you please leave my cabin; go through the details and get back, and this time if I don't have answers, I WILL KILL YOU ALL!"

Like lost heroes, we returned to our desks, wondering what we had done in our life to end up here. All of us were tired, not showing the slightest interest; we called it a day and left office.

The next day, we had a meeting, comprising of three mentally tortured monkeys, on how to tackle the lion.

The ring master came up with an idea, which resulted in a second rule which was, 'From now on, whatever the situation, whatever the circumstances, we will meet the lion only in the afternoons!'

Reason? After a heavy lunch, the mind goes off to sleep.

All of us were happy with this decision and started the day with a positive note.

Trrngg…trrngg… *Oh no! The dreaded call…*

"Yes sir, yeah he has read it… yes sir, we will be there right away," I said.

"Okay guys, Doctor is calling; are you done with the document thing?" I looked at Vicky.

"Oh no, what is this? It's not even been twelve hours since he roasted us. How can he expect us to read this document?" cribbed Vicky.

"No problem yaar, don't worry I will handle it," Ring master said.

Now, having no choice, all three of us got ready to meet the 'Doctor'.

We usually had to announce our status near our cubicle - stating our availability or otherwise. Since all the three of us were invited for the royal meeting with our CEO, our status message read something like this- 'FUNERAL'.

"Hmmmmm... so you guys are ready? Have you read this?"

We humbly looked at Vicky.

"Sir… yes sir… I have read it…"

"Okay so what material have they specified?"

"I… I... think admiralty brass…"

"What the hell? Admiralty brass for this service? Are you sure you have read it?"

"Yeah… no… um...one sec sir, I will just refer…"

Well, do I need to tell you readers the rest?

"Bloody hell! What? You still haven't read this? High time you people do some work!"

Now, casting his eyes upon us he asked, "Have you people bothered to look into this?"

Me: no answer.

Ring master: no answer.

At this point, Doctor got angry and twisted his hand as if strangling Vicky.

"Ha ha… cough, cough," Vicky laughed, and then somehow managed to muffle the laugh.

"Ha ha ha ha…" I laughed aloud and dashed out of the room.

'Ring master' just looked at us to say we had to control ourselves else we'd be thrown out of this place.

I immediately went back to him and apologized for my behaviour. He simply nodded showing least interest and continued blasting Vicky for not having read the document.

So this is how we usually started and ended our days here in this so-called design office!

If this was not enough, we had a bunch more to handle and the description of these species is enough to inform of our plights. I will go by the hierarchy.

Doctor: This species is not found commonly on earth; it has come from a far of land where not knowing any information is equivalent to committing a crime. This species is highly active during the day time and it gradually decreases post lunch, will not attack until and unless provoked, will get provoked very easily for no reason and for all reasons. Quiet, wrinkled and old in appearance, but, 'don't judge the book by the cover', is my advice after spending three years with this species. "Bloody hell…!"

Word of caution: Stay away as much as possible; has a higher attraction rate than a magnet and tends to behave like a leech!

Mr. Suryakiran (Hyena): Let me introduce you to this character; he heads the engineering world, is highly restless and behaves like a drunken monkey with or without provoking, has a highly suspicious character and might end up keeping a surveillance camera on every desk!

Word of caution: 'Always smile; you never know who is falling in love… Oops, I mean…who is watching your every move!'

Mr. Nandkishore (Jackal): This is another species that heads the finance world; so far we haven't dealt with this species, but he possesses one or two of the above-mentioned characters.

Word of caution: The word 'money' can make you see its true colours! So don't mention it when you are near this species.

Read on to find out the deadly lot…

The engineering department is no less than a drama stage.

Characters involved: Mr. Sudesh (Engineering head): Local name - Parasite.

Mr. Ranganathan (Deputy engineering head): Local name – *Betala*.

Mr. Swami (Engineering consultant): Local name – Wise old owl.

General scene in the department.

"Whaat saar… how can we do this now? I have to finish the assembly drawing by today; give me sometime at least," complained Praveen, walking behind *Betala*.

"What can I do? It's not in my hands; you have to ask the higher ups," said *Betala* adjusting his big glasses.

Praveen walked away with a long face swearing that he would go in search of a new job.

All of us understood his plight and nodded in agreement.

"Acha, Giri, what is theese, gate valve shown here? What does it dooo?" crooned the parasite standing near Giri's table.

A bunch of people giggled and started calling Giri's name.

"Sir, this is a gate valve. It's called 'gate' because it has characteristics similar to a gate, that is, it opens and closes. It is mainly used for water purposes," answered Giri, looking up from the monitor.

"Anything else?" he asked.

"No, no, thank you so much for your help; *acha, beta*, do you know Excel?"

"Sir, I know Excel, excel-lently; what do you want?"

"Oh, nice, nice; please come to my chamber and see; I have prepared an Excel sheet. I'm not able to add the formulae."

"Simple sir, I will just teach you in two minutes," said Giri and walked into the chamber making a face.

"Ha ha ha ha… Ho ho… no no… *acha*, he he he. Very nice sir, pleasure talking to you." Suddenly everyone was amused to hear this kind of laughter from the parasite's room. We all laughed giving the old man some company.

"You see, when I was working with them, I had a similar situation; the nozzle placement is very important and the load calculation should be properly checked," said the old wise owl talking to Nikhil.

"Okay sir, so what do you suggest I do now?" asked Nikhil impatiently.

"What we did that time is calculating the stress…"

"Sir, I want a solution…" Now Nikhil's patience was tested more than enough.

"See, you should understand one thing; I am a consultant here. I can give only suggestions; you have to look for an answer," said the old owl, sternly.

"Okay sir, thank you for the help. I will talk to *Betala*… oops, will talk to Mr. Ranga and decide." He came out nodding his head.

"Sir, may I come in?"

Betala suddenly got up. "Oh… who… yeah, yeah, please come." He suppressed his yawn and welcomed Nikhil.

"Sir, I have a doubt; this is regarding the nozzle loads. Can you please tell me how should I calculate?"

"Let me see, okay, so what is your question?" *Betala* asked looking at the bundle of sheets in front of him.

"Do you still jump from branch to branch when Vikrama comes to catch you?"

"Pardon me?"

"Sir, I mean, do we have to take any branch connections from the pipe or not?"

"Oh that, hmm… have you done any previous project similar to this?"

"No sir, this is the…"

"Why don't you do one thing; just go to the library and find out if we had executed similar jobs before. You see, that will clear all your doubts," said Betala half pushing the sheets back to Nikhil.

Frustrated, Nikhil gathered the sheets and stormed out of the room, and decided to go to parasite.

"Excuse me sir, can I take five minutes of your time?"

"Oh please come in dear; how are you?" smiled the parasite showing his fake set of teeth.

"Very fine, thank you sir; how are you?"

"I'm always good; you see, in Mahabharata when Arjuna..."

"Sir, I have a doubt."

"Oh yeah, please tell, when Arjuna had a doubt he went to..."

"S-I-R, this is regarding the nozzle load calculation; can you please look into it?"

"Oh *acha*, is it? Okay. What project is this?"

"This is for an export job."

"Where is this nozzle coming?"

On my head! "Sir, this nozzle is located on the exchanger..."

"*Acha*; so what does this exchanger do?"

"Sir, exchanger will perform its duty, I want you to check the nozzles."

"Wait *na*; I should understand completely; then only I will be able to help you."

"Sir this nozzle has to bear a certain amount of stress; I want you to check..."

"*Acha*, did you talk to Mr. Swami regarding this?"

"Yes sir, I have checked it with Mr. Swami and Ranga; both of them are confused, so I came to you."

"Well... why don't you do one thing? You talk to Mr. Swami and tell me..."

"Thank you very much sir, I think I need to do it myself." Nikhil's temper had crossed limits and he decided to talk to the 'Furnace'.

"Hello mam, is Doctor free? Can I meet him?" Nikhil called Doctor's secretary to ask for an appointment.

"Allo, who is this?" In a heavy Malyali accent replied Sridevi, Doctor's fifty-year-old secretary.

"Mam, this is Nikhil from the engineering department. I..."

"Oh... you people are so lucky; I have to struggle here...always *Dactar* calling me; I having no time *vonly* to *respire...*"

"Mam, is Doctor free?"

"Wait, I will check and tell you."

After five minutes...

"Yes he is *freea*; come after *onne 'our,*" replied the secretary.

Then she rambled, "You know how much I work *ya...* I..."

"Thank you m'am," Nikhil said and slammed the phone.

After one hour...

"Hmmmmm... What is it about?" Doctor Rao looked at him with the double lens glass.

"Sir, about nozzle loads," Nikhil said, half sitting out of the chair.

"Okay, this calculation is very important; if we don't mention the loads, then the nozzle may not withstand the forces..."

"Yes sir, that's the reason I am asking your guidance."

"Okay let us see... what is the fluid?"

"Sir, water..."

"What do you mean water? I know its water! I am asking you the quality. Is it de-min water or sea water?"

"Sir, de-min water."

"Okay, now what size have you mentioned?"

"Four inches, sir."

"What is the flow rate of water?"

"Sir, fifteen cubic meters per hour."

"Okay, now how do you calculate the flow through circular ducts?"

"Sir... I ... think we should take... area of circle."

"Then?"

"Then..." Nikhil looked down at his books and started searching if such an equation existed...

"What sort of a mechanical engineer are you?"

"Sir... I..."

"Why can't you people answer such simple questions? We are not doing rocket science here. One equation and you think so much. How will you design the entire equipment?"

"Sir... I..."

"Okay, do you know what does ASME code section 8 say?"

"Sir, I will get that book; one minu..."

"What do you mean you will get the book? Can't you remember what you people read everyday? What sort of engineers India is producing?" Doctor was literally red and Nikhil felt as if a volcano was ready to erupt any second.

"Now will you answer or gape at me?" Doctor's voice echoed in the silent corridor of the third floor, meant for highly respected executives.

"I... I... know it, but have forgotten..." Nikhil, by now, had lost his speech too.

"I think I need to talk to your head and check what is wrong with you people. Earlier, I had some bunch of monkeys here with the same kind of face. This is no kindergarten school, my dear, this is office; you need to be well aware of what goes in." Doctor shook his head wondering where he had landed.

"Sir, I think the code says we should take ten percent excess stress and calculate." Nikhil somehow managed to utter a few words.

"Is it? *Haan*? Bloody, since how many years are you working in this field? Charlies! I tell you, useless charlies!"

Hearing this, our MD, Mr. Hyena, barged into the cabin and yelled, "What the hell is happening here?"

Nikhil was very tensed and tried to talk, but was interrupted by Doctor who said, "He doesn't know A DAMN THING, SURI. What is your department doing, I say!"

Hyena felt insulted and looked at Nikhil angrily demanding an explanation for this insult.

He almost looked like Ambreesh Puri in the movie Mr. India.

Nikhil collected his documents and said, "Sir, I actually wanted to ask … wanted to calculate... nozzle loads…"

"You fool! Don't you know we never do this kind of calculations here? We always outsource these calculations!"

Oh! Nikhil's face was worth a watch; he came to the engineering floor and dumped his files. "What is wrong with this company yaar! Bloody, for one calculation, they are making us run from pillar to post."

So here is a small snippet on how things work in our system. Here you won't learn what to do, but certainly you will learn what not to do!

CHAPTER 2
IN SOUP

"Wow, so cool man," I exclaimed happily looking at the mail.

"What happened? Why you so excited?" Zahir peeped into my PC.

"Dear all, I request the below mentioned staff to get ready for a technical meeting with the customers in China," I read it aloud so that all the three of us could hear. "And the first name is… Mr. Vikram Pundit!"

"From Chandini Chowk to China…" I started singing looking at Vicky.

"Oh come on, guys, it's only China. Stop behaving like this," he said.

"Hey, it seems you get to pick your food there like shrimps, crabs, octopus… is it true? And there are no termites or reptiles left in the country as a majority of them end up in the human belly!" I asked him trying hard not to laugh.

"Again food! Madam, is there anything else on your mind?" Zahir looked at me shaking his head.

"You see, boss, I live to eat. I think you have heard of it," I told him with a smile.

"Now that you mention, I am a little worried about my food. What do I eat there?" Our vegetarian friend became thoughtful.

"MTR *hain na*, manage *karlo*," Zahir said.

"I think that is my only resort," Vicky said cheering up.

So our Vicky was finally going to the 'Land of Dragons and Emperors'. The D-day arrived and before he left, I gave him a list of items to download from the China market. Even though he would be gone only for a week, we still missed him.

All the while I was thinking about what gifts I might get when he returns. Day in and out I would discuss with Zahir, but, of course, I would get the usual blank look.

One week passed without our dear friend and I was eagerly waiting for his return.

And the next Monday, Vicky arrived from the 'Land of noodles' (now don't tell me I'm thinking about food again; it's easy to relate, don't you think?).

Our hero arrived at noon with a huge bag.

"Welcome back, Vicky," Zahir said as he hugged him.

"Welcome back, buddy," I said with a nice smile.

"Hi guys, how have you been?" he said dumping his luggage.

"Hey man, you have lost oodles of weight. What have you done to yourself? Please give me some tips," I asked him aloud.

"No food and all work can make you virtually slim; take my suggestion," Zahir pulled my leg.

"Huh, moron; anyways Vicky, start off; how was your trip? How did the discussions go?" I pulled my chair and sat next to Vicky.

"Yeah boss, fill us with the details; how did it go? Was it fruitful?" Zahir joined me.

"Well guys, I had an awesome time there, but I had to make some basic sacrifice like FOOD, you see," he said looking at me.

"My God, that's criminal; that's a total *atayachar* to your belly. No wonder you look in good shape now," I said grinning.

"I will pour out the details; just give me a few seconds to breathe."

"We started at midnight on Sunday, all the four of us seated in the economy class."

"Oh, economy class?" I asked Vicky sarcastically.

"Madam, they wouldn't mind dumping us in lower class or even cargo, if available!"

"Ha ha ha, sorry, continue," I laughed, imagining Vicky seated in the cargo section next to huge cartons.

"Okay, now I will proceed, with your permission madam," Vicky said looking at me.

"Sure buddy, we are all ears!" I said in full *josh*.

"Okay, so we started our journey; it was an eight hour trip, quite a pleasant one."

"So what about the air hostesses?" Zahir gave Vicky a wicked smile.

"I will tell you, but not here; not in front of ladies," he said looking at me.

"Who ladies? Come on yaar, don't be a spoil sport, tell me," I pestered Vicky.

"I say eight and a half; now nobody shall interrupt me or else I will not proceed," he said winking at Zahir.

"We reached Hong Kong airport at about eleven in the morning. Then we had to catch another flight to Shanghai; we reached at about three in the evening, and were ushered by a smart woman in her mid-twenties. Fortunately she spoke in English, which was such a relief to know. In China, people hardly speak English. She dropped us in a nice three star hotel. We didn't do anything much that day, just took rest in our rooms. For dinner, we were taken to a small quaint restaurant.

We four, along with that Chinese woman who had come with us for assistance, sat at a huge arc-shaped mahogany table .We were given a fifty-page menu! Not a single item was vegetarian except for vegetables and fruits. All the four of us being teetotallers, ended up having some fruit salad, but had difficulty in having the ice cream; they had put a dash of red jelly and so many other things, we double checked to make sure it was really vegetarian and not some animal product. Food as I mentioned was horrible.

I must tell you one thing; The Chinese are very cordial people, probably one of the best I have seen. The Chinese lady, her name was Chio Wang (pronounced as shi-yo Wang), was really hurt that she couldn't offer us good food. Throughout the day she kept on apologizing for the inconvenience."

"Did you shop anything for us?" I demanded Vicky.

"This is for you," said Vicky taking out a very cute teddy bear from his bag.

"Oh... cho chweet, thanks a lot," I crooned, clutching the doll tight.

"And this is for you sir," he gave a golden box to Zahir.

"Thanks dude, what is this…" he said opening the box. He let out a whistle as soon as he saw a leather belt. "Cool man, nice one."

Since Vicky was on the verge of getting married, we all started teasing him.

"Yeah, I got a jade necklace for her," he blushed with a smile.

"Nice one," I said.

"The Chinese are harmonious, hardworking and warm people," started off Vicky.

"Yeah right! Do you know what's happening in the Indo-China border? Are they exchanging pleasantries?" I snorted angrily.

"Look yaar, politics apart, they are peace-loving folk," Vicky supported them. Realizing it's a delicate subject, he drifted to the topic of Chinese culture.

"They have a very rich culture similar to ours. Though we don't abide by most of them, they follow them stringently."

He continued, "In China, the festivals are celebrated with great pomp and show. They have many festivals like spring festival, lantern festival, and ya, Christmas too."

"And what about *Chinese chicks*?" Zahir asked.

"Oh, they were great! But there is only one problem; I couldn't differentiate one from another; they all look alike. Since it was snowing at this time of the year, apart from the half closed eyes, I couldn't get any other view," he giggled.

"I've heard the Chinese are superstitious; is it true?" I inquired.

"Man-oh-man, don't mention about that; I had a terrible time understanding them. You know, the first day when I reached the site, I was sporting an evening beard and a moustache. Though it wasn't prominent, I was being stared at constantly by the people there. Then unable to control my curiosity, I asked one of them in sign language; he explained to me that having a moustache is considered bad luck!

"I was taken aback, didn't know what to do. Should I wear a *burhka* now? You won't believe what they did. They gave me a razor and asked me politely to shave it off!"

"Ha ha ha, so they were working right under your nose *haan*?" I taunted.

"That's not all, they asked me how many drawings I have got. I said 'four'; a mere mention of that harmless number got me cold stares. If not for the interpreter, they would have put me into their turbines!"

"Oh why?" Zahir and I asked in unison.

"The word 'four', sounding like the word for death, is not to be uttered. Death and dying are never mentioned. Since I had uttered those un-utter-able words, I had to apologize! Then I took a vow never to talk until asked and not even when asked!"

"Even clipping toenails or fingernails at night is bad luck; the person will be visited by a ghost."

"Ah now I know why we have such people in our office," I said pointing at *Betala*. "Vicky must be clipping toe nails at night," I teased Vicky.

Undeterred by the remarks, Vicky continued, "But otherwise they are nice people; though they tend to be conservative, they are friendly."

"Okay Vicky, tell me what's the difference between Chinese and Japanese. They look like lost twins. See, both of them are short statured, and have non-existent eyes, and they are yellow!" Zahir quipped.

"Japanese come from Japan and Chinese from China!" Vicky started slapping his thigh for this on-your-face joke.

"Now come on guys, just because I went to China doesn't mean I have done research on them! Don't ask me such questions. If you really are interested, why don't you Google? I'm very sure thousands out there are under the same confusion!"

"What about their food habits?"

"Don't ask me, It's horrible… they have this huge aquarium with lots of snakes, sea animals, and what not; I don't know how people eat them. In fact I saw people relishing 'blood'!" he said with a disgusted look on his face.

"Blood! They belong to Dracula groups or what?" I too was equally horrified to hear this. Just the thought of gulping blood made me sick in the stomach.

"And that's not all; eating Chinese food is like a balancing act. With two slender sticks, you have to eat the noodles and it keeps slipping off every time you pick a strand. One strand of noodles took approximately ten minutes and after the juggling act; the result? I tasted a bland string which seemed like a thick thread boiled with water! All this for sticks!"

"Imagine eating chapatti or dosa or idly with the sticks!" I said.

"Oh yeah dear, you can try; probably that will help you lose some weight. By the time you pick the grains and munch on them, it will take your entire day!" Zahir teased me.

"Then proceed, Vicky..." I said ignoring Zahir with a 'huh'.

"By the way, what about the Gobi Manchurian? Did you find them?"I asked.

"That's a misconception yaar; it has got nothing to do with Chinese cuisine. It's more like an Indian dish with a Chinese touch."

"Oh! I was wondering how they can prepare something that is so tasty; now it's clear to me," I said appearing smarter.

"They believe in 'WASTE NOT AND WANT NOT'."

"Oh! Is that the reason why they don't even spare the smallest of creatures and reptiles?" Zahir asked cheekily.

The questioning session went on for the whole day. We attacked him with all sorts of questions, till he was so dead tired that he had to plead to us to let go of him.

So we finally finished our 'Coffee with Karan' session and let poor Vicky go home.

CHAPTER 3
SLAM BOOK DAYS

It was a month since Vicky's return from China, and by now, we had enough details about China, so we had stopped bothering him.

Vicky, Zahir and I were sipping cappuccino and munching on fries in our office canteen.

"Bagged the order *haan*, great!" Vicky said with a glint of triumph.

"Ya, don't know what *chamatkar* you guys did in China to bag this order. Bloody, those people are not that easy to woo. Seriously, what did you guys do there?" Zahir caught Vicky on this one.

"V for Vicky; V for victory," started off Vicky.

"Yeah yeah, those people; I'm sure they were out of their minds to sign this deal. Anyways, quite an achievement considering the kind of preparation and presentation," I added agreeing with Zahir.

"Come on yaar, don't take away the credit. It wasn't a cake walk for us, we gave our 100 percent, to be able to get this order," Vicky defended himself.

"We know; just pulling your leg," I smiled and asked Zahir to get something to eat.

"So Vicky tell me, what about your treat? When are you taking us out?" Zahir asked him.

"Yeah you better! But, we decide the venue," I demanded.

"Okay, okay guys, tomorrow is an 'off', right, so let's meet at six in the evening and then have dinner."

Next day, Zahir and I reached the venue and asked Vicky to join us.

"Oh no yaar, please don't do this to me; I am seriously done with this," Vicky started to complain the minute he saw us.

"What did we do? What happened? Don't behave like this. People will think we are harassing you," Zahir tried to calm Vicky down.

"You people na… useless! I tell you, absolutely! Out of all places in the world you had to choose this God forsaken place!"

Zahir and I started laughing uncontrollably.

"Oh god it hurts… my, my… What would we do without you Vicks?" I said holding my stomach.

"Anything is okay, but not a Chinese restaurant again!" Vicky was literally angry with us. We had deliberately chosen a Chinese restaurant just to tick off Vicky and it had worked perfectly for us!

"Okay, since I'm happy, I will not kill you guys." Vicky finally controlled his anger.

"Ha ha ha… *Saale*... V for Victory *haan*, now V for Vanquish," Zahir mocked.

"Okay, order fast and let's get out of this place."

We finally ordered and started eating, and suddenly I saw that Zahir was not a part of our conversation. He sat very silent and withdrawn. He was eyeing a girl sitting diagonal to us. She was a pretty girl, and one could see her bountiful tresses as she laughed throwing her head back. There were some guys on the other table who were also ogling at her.

"*Kahin pe nigha hain, kahin pe nishana...*"I started humming.

"Uh... Sorry... did you say something?" Zahir looked at us blankly.

"So what's with that girl?" I asked him.

"Who... which girl...?" Zahir tried to look innocent.

"We saw that and you are caught red-handed ..."

"She... resembles one of my old friends, so I was just looking at her, that's it. Guys, now stop staring at me as if I have some hidden secrets. I don't have any, you get that!"

"Ooohh... Somebody is serious *haan!* Definitely the matter runs deep down till here," I said pointing at his heart.

"Now you guys want some beating from me."

"Nah... it's okay... it happens to everyone you see... even Vicky couldn't propose to that Chinese female." I tried to lighten the matter.

After this, we ate silently. We knew there was something about that girl that had triggered our dear 'Ring master'.

We finished our dinner and left the place. I set off with Zahir to my place. Zahir had a stern face and hardly spoke to me; he didn't even play his favourite music, so I sat looking outside the window and I wondered what had happened. He dropped me near my PG and drove away. I decided not to bother him' maybe he was disturbed about something. With a sigh, I walked towards my room.

Next morning, I saw Zahir. He did not seem fine; he appeared withdrawn.

"Hi buddy, everything fine?" I asked Zahir.

"Yes."

"So what happened? What is bothering you? Just let it out."

"What are you talking about? Don't make such a big hue and cry about this. I'm absolutely fine!"

"This is too much; I know you are hurt. It's written on your damn face!"

Zahir started to say something and stopped; he turned away and rested his head on his hand.

"Hmmm that girl resembled someone; old wounds are back. I'm sorry for behaving like this but I'm in no good shape."

"I know; that is why I'm asking you to talk about it. It will make you feel better, trust me," I said looking concerned.

But he stood still; I turned back to my computer and started working. Just to rejuvenate, I asked Zahir about his college life.

"Come on now, you can share; we are best friends right?" I coaxed him.

"Now don't do *nakhra;* come let's go to the cafeteria; we will eat and chat," I said with a smile on the face.

"Eating should be a synonym for your name, seriously," Zahir said as we moved towards the cafeteria.

"I want spinach and corn sandwich; what about you?"

I asked Zahir, looking at the bright orange coloured menu.

"Get something yaar, anything will do," he said and sat on the sofa facing the water fountain.

I got the tray and laid down the food items in front of Zahir.

"Okay, so tell me from the beginning, and I 'wanfu' hear even 'abouf' your 'crufhes'," I said with a mouthful of sandwich.

"Okay, I studied in a place called Belgaum nearly eighty kilometres from my home town, Dharwad. Belgaum is a small town, not yet developed into a major city. It's a land with great traditional values and even the locals there are very simple minded, yet very helpful.

Considering my stupendous performance in Common Entrance Test, I could manage a decent seat in an engineering college. But since I had no choice of subject, I had to take the tabooed branch 'Chemical Engineering'. I left my house with the same old crying scene with mom. I told them it's just a two-hour drive from home, but it was no use; their tears didn't dry that soon. Anyways, with the help of my maternal uncle, I got a place in the medical hostel. With a piece of advice on how to behave, etc., my uncle took leave.

I wandered here and there looking at the old buildings wondering if I could find a hideout. My thoughts were interrupted by a group of people who were smoking. "Hey you! Are you a fresher?" I looked at them and wondered whether I should confront or surrender. Seeing their strength, I decided on the latter. "Yes, I have joined newly; I am Pashas' nephew."

"I don't care whose nephew or whose husband you are, just answer my questions!" one of guys smirked at me.

"Okay," I said meekly.

"Since it's your first day, you will be spared; tomorrow morning, we will explain you the rules."

"Okay," I said and went to my room.

I shared my room with two people - Imitiaz and Harish. We exchanged 'hellos' and spoke casually about each others' family. I think we went to sleep immediately as neither had any topic nor subject to continue the conversation.

Next day, in the morning, I asked Imitiaz, "Where is the washroom?"

"Go straight and turn left," he replied busily gazing at the newspaper.

Muttering 'thanks', I carried my toothbrush and a towel and stepped out of the room. Well, I couldn't find any friendly faces but still some people greeted me. Finally I saw the wash room, or should I mention, the 'washrooms', consisting of ten bath rooms.

'Oh man! Should I bathe here? I might become more dirty looking at the bathroom,' I thought, but had no choice you see; I had to go through all this. I was about to step into one of them when suddenly, somebody pushed me hard from behind. It was one of the guys who had seen me last night. 'Oh shit! Now what does he want.'

"*Saale,* didn't I tell you that certain rules have to be followed here!" he thundered.

"What did I do now? Should I take your permission to take bath or when I answer Nature's call?" I asked, sounding equally angry.

"*Baap re baap*, look at you, teeny weenie creature not even been a day since you joined, talking to a senior like this!" he approached me menacingly.

"*Bhai*, he is a new comer. I will explain the rules to him." Suddenly Imitiaz butted in between me and that *bhai*.

"*Theek hain;* make sure he knows where he stands in front of seniors like us." He gave me one of those 'I will kill you' looks and entered the bathroom.

"What sort of a rule is this? Should I take bath with others' permission? Bloody, I have also paid my hostel fees and I deserve an equal share of everything," I said rather angrily as Imitiaz showed me another bathroom.

"See, they are seniors and the first and foremost thing you have to learn is to obey them and always allow your seniors to take whatever they want; got it?" Imitiaz told me in a brotherly way.

"Okay, but ..."

"No 'buts', finish off your bath soon. Even I have to take a bath and remember we have to catch a bus today, so hurry up!" Imitiaz closed my door and went off.

We finished our breakfast with loud burps and walked towards the bus stop.

Since it was my first day, Imitiaz accompanied me till the bus stop. He was from the medical college and was well aware of the place.

"Your bus comes here. You just wait. I have a class now; got to leave; hope you don't mind," he said and walked away.

"I saw two people standing near the stop, so I approached them and asked, "K.M.E College?" They looked at me as if I had committed a crime and replied, "No, G.E.T, your rival college." 'Okies! Got the message,' I thought and waited till the bus arrived."

"So no one ragged you in the bus? Were there no seniors?" I asked him sipping my dried up 'diet coke'.

"Seniors were there but not the *khatharnak* types; just a few mild ones occupying the last seats. The middle seats were empty, so I occupied one of them. I sat there looking forward to seeing my new college."

"I got off the bus and smiled at the sight of college. There were four or five buildings that formed a semicircle, and at the centre, there was a huge water fountain that looked unattended. Both sides of the buildings were masked by huge trees, and the breeze being on its high, they swayed to and fro as if welcoming me into this world. I was really happy to see the college; it looked decent. I walked towards the administrator's office where I became friendly with one of the guys I met, Roopak Patel.

Both of us were struggling with our forms and decided to seek some help. I looked up and found a girl filling a form. I approached her and asked if she could help us. She looked up; I must admit she was very pretty. I know I'm sounding a bit filmy, but she was pretty. She was wearing a blood red *salwar* and had tied her hair in a neat ponytail. She smiled and helped us with the form.

"Not bad, there are some good birds here," I said and winked at Roopak. "Dude, it's the first day; we better get to our classes," he said.

We headed towards the 'chemical department' and since

it was the first semester, we had a common syllabus. And we had to share our class with 'bio-medical' students.

"Wow, sixty percent girls!" I exclaimed as I sat next to Roopak in the fourth or fifth row.

Then the classes started with the usual "I am so and so..."

I went back to my hostel and both my room mates were busy with a human skull. They looked as if they were practicing some voodoo or black magic.

"What are you guys doing with that skull?" I asked them.

"We have to study the structure; tomorrow we have a seminar where we have to present our study," Imitiaz said looking deep into the empty eye socket of the skull.

"This is a woman's skull. You can see the..."Harish started explaining to me.

"Boss, please keep me out of your skull business," I said.

'Man! Whom do I share the rooms with? ...creepy,' I thought and left them to themselves romancing the skull!

The next day, I caught the bus and sat in the last seat gazing at everyone.

At the next stop, about five or six seniors got in. In the first semester, whether you announce it or not, but 'FRESHER' is written on your face. I presumed this because as soon as they saw me, they came like a pack of hungry wolves.

"So, what is your name, fresher?" said one of them.

"Zahir Pathan." I tried to look bold.

"So you are a cross of Zahir Khan and Irfan Pathan, is it?" They mentioned few cricketers' names and started laughing.

"No," I simply stated.

"Bloody, with every sentence you have to address us with 'sir'."

"Sorry sir," I said with a lot of humiliation.

"And my dear friend, bear in mind to always look at the third button of your shirt when you talk to us," another wolf growled.

"Okay Zahir Khan, when is your birthday?"

"Sir, it's Zahir Pathan," I said.

"Whatever Zahir, now answer."

"Sir, it's 17th October."

"Why not celebrate it today? Cut the cake and distribute it to everyone," someone from behind ordered me.

"Sir, but where is the cake?" I looked perplexed.

"You asshole! How dare you back answer seniors?" They yanked my bag, took out a new book and tore a page out of it.

"Now cut this and distribute it to the group of girls sitting in the front and remember you have to get a gift from them."

All of them sneered at my plight.

I was asked not to use my brain and if I did, have one I didn't bother activating. So sincerely, I went to the girls and was both happy and embarrassed; it was the same girl who had helped me with my admission form. She smiled as soon as she saw me.

I said, "Please take this cake; it's my birthday." She giggled and said, "Okay, it's those boys again and you are the target is it?" I smiled nervously eyeing both the parties. It was like beauty and the beasts.

Anyways, she gave me a rupee as a gift. I was relived that my stupid act could generate some cash. And now, the wolves started clapping and said, "Well done boy; I thought you will not obey us. Welcome to our college. If you need any help, ask us; we are always there." They spoke as if I had done some great deed.

"Hi, I am Rashmi," she said as soon as we got down from the bus.

"Uh... hi I am Zahir." I purposely didn't reveal my last name after that bus incident.

"Thanks for the gift," I told her with a smile.

"Don't bother; I know these people. I am in mechanical first sem, you are in...?"

'Mechanical, strange,' I thought, 'It's meant to be for 'mean-man-world', not for pretty and delicate girls.'

"Chemical," I said hoping I wouldn't get any typical, 'Why chemical? No scope you see', but she just smiled and said, "Mine is the third building; I guess yours is the next one. I'll catch you in the evening." She waved and said, "Bye."

Rashmi and I started getting close. Now don't have any ideas," he said, looking at me while I was still toying with the menu.

"Who? Me? Oh please! I am not like you. Waiter I want one *samosa*. Then what happened?" I asked more curiously now.

"The semester started with 'hi's' and 'hellos'. We formed groups amongst ourselves. I became close to Roopak. He is among those who could make girls burn out with jealousy. He had the most enviable figure, almost at par with girls. I would tease him, "Roopu, at this rate forget about getting a girl friend; you are not even eligible to look at them!"

Both of us had a mission; mine was searching for a girl friend and his was body building.

By the end of my first year, my group had been formed - Roopak Patel, Tabrez Tamategar (Tubbs), Aftar Hasan, Sachin Ghadekar (SG) and Praveen Kapoor Chaurasia (PKC).

Tubbs is one such character whose middle name is trouble. He sets his foot and you know for sure that trouble is around the corner. Not to mention he actually looked like one.

PKC and SG have no distinguishable characters!

Oh, man, I have to tell you this… it was so funny, we… forget us, the entire college used to laugh when they used to see SG. This guy was an ardent movie buff; movies that define their age and thoughts. So his abbreviation was just perfectly associated with his ways, Zahir continued at the mention of his friends.

"It all happened in the fourth semester; SG had missed an entire week and there was no communication from him. So we decided to call his parents and find out.

I dialled the number and waited for someone to answer the phone.

"Hello," someone answered.

"Uh hello, uncle? I am Zahir here," I said recognizing SG's fathers voice.

"Hello *beta*, how are you?"

"I'm fine uncle, how are you doing? And by the way,

is Sachin there?" There was a slight sigh on the other side.

"Uncle is everything okay?" I asked.

"*Beta*, please note down the address and come here; you can see him yourself - 24th main, opposite post office, City Central Hospital, Ward number 34. It's a red coloured building, just across the city market."

I hung up immediately and rushed to the hospital wondering what could have happened to this fellow.

I reached the hospital and went straight to the room.

I saw him lying down on a white bed, with a big bandage on his head and there was a glucose drip attached to his arm; he was awake and staring at the roof.

I was still standing at the door and was trying to assess the situation.

Suddenly he pointed his finger at the roof as if he just declared someone out in a cricket match and asked, "What is that?" His brother went next to him and tried to look from the same angle.

"That is a cobweb, Peeku," he said lovingly to his brother.

'Peeku! What a nick name! He has never told us about this. I will have to tell my friends,' I thought.

"You moron! What is that shinning on the web?"

"That is light," he said.

"Do you know who invented it?" he asked in a very serious tone.

"No, I don't remember," replied his brother.

I was watching this interesting conversation standing near the door. Suddenly he looked at me and said, "Zahir, mere *bhai*, come here, sit with me," he said, pointing towards the metal chair next to his bed. The chair squeaked noisily as soon as I sat, the only noise in that room apart from his mother's sniffs.

"Can you please tell me what it is?" He asked the same question again. Since I was aware of the previous episode, I said, "Thomas Alva Edison."

"You idiot, I was asking about the fan. I don't repeat my questions," he declared.

"My dear friend, who are all these people around me? They seem so stupid," he said looking at me. I was in a shock and went numb for a few seconds, not knowing what to say. I couldn't utter a single word.

"What? Uncle? What happened to him? How did it happen?" I said looking at his father.

"*Beta*, Sachin met with an accident and he was in ICU. Today they shifted him to the general ward and the doctor said he has temporarily lost his memory and it might take a few days to get it back. I am at loss to understand how he remembered your name," a dejected voice answered.

'Oh shucks! Why me out of all the people in this world!' I wanted to say, but stayed quiet. I had borrowed a thousand bucks from him last month and this would have helped me. Now I would not have to return it back. I was still thinking about these things when he called me again.

"Zahir, do you see that lady in the opposite bed?" he said pointing at a 25-something-year-old young lady sleeping with her hands bandaged.

"Yeah I do," I said wondering what he wanted to say.

"You know, we are distant relatives." I looked at uncle

and their family members; uncle just lifted his hands up as if to say only God can save them and aunty ran outside wiping her tears with her *pallu* and his brother too joined her.

'Now what am I supposed to do.' I was left alone in the room with this guy. Before I could even react, I saw two of my friends rushing in the room; it was PKC and Tubbs. "*Yaar* what happened?" *Kya huwa*? Did he meet with an accident?" they asked in a hurried tone.

I hushed them and took them to the side and explained the situation.

"*Saala*, never in his life he bothered who discovered him; *abhi ye fan beech main kahan agaya?*" Tubbs said.

"*Yaar*, please be quiet; even I don't know how to handle this. Can you guys get some doctor? His family is worried," I said.

"Oye, they should be happy; he was such a menace…"

"Please *yaar*, not now… be a little serious," I tried telling them. "Look who is talking? You were the one who made us laugh at the old watchman's funeral, right?"

"*Abbey yaar*, look at him, who will cry …" In any other situation, I would have completely agreed with Tubbs, but at this point, I was stupefied at his condition.

"Zahir, what are you doing with those beggars? Come here."

I started to laugh, but controlled myself. Looking at PKC's reaction, I said, "Please go fetch a doctor …" I diverted any further such direct remarks which were true in every sense.

"Come here; I was telling you about that girl *na*, she is my distant…"

"I know she is your relative, then what next?" I interrupted.

"Bloody, who told you she is my relative? She is my distant friend. You know why she is sleeping there?"

I said I didn't know, not wanting him to start off his 'distant' story again.

"I fought with her and won the game; that's why she is not talking to me." At this point, he absolutely made no sense to me, so without bothering too much, I went out to look at 'those beggars'… Oops… my friends.

They were coming along with a senior doctor. I heaved a sigh of relief as soon as I saw them.

"Doctor, why is he talking like this? What has happened to him? And he remembers only Zahir's name and does not recognize anyone… why so?"

"This is a very peculiar case, umm… it's better we discuss this in my cabin." We followed the doctor leaving SG alone in his room.

"Umm… have you heard of amnesia?" asked Dr. Anuj Saxena. He was a middle aged man with receding hair, and had warmth in his eyes that made us feel SG was in good hands.

"Amnesia refers to a temporary memory loss. This can occur due to various reasons like too much of alcohol consumption, or due to any trauma, stress, as you must be aware. It can also be due to accidents. Luckily your friend didn't damage his head.

The condition of your friend is called 'Fugue state'; this is a temporary memory loss. This occurs due to some sudden accident. There is nothing to worry about; he will be back to normal in a few days. But what I want from you is total support. It's good that he recognizes one of you and now it's up to you young man, to get him back," he said, looking at me in anticipation.

"And one more thing; here, the patient may repeat the same things, so I suggest you develop some patience," he said patting me on my back and left for his usual rounds.

Everyone turned to look at me in a slow motion. I felt the whole world had fallen on my tender shoulders.

'Bloody, I'm no doctor here; what the hell am I supposed to do?'

"So, are you going to help our *Ghajini baba?*" Tubbs asked referring to the recent movie in which the hero suffered from memory loss.

"*Yaar*, I'm tensed; what should I tell him?" I was worried now. My friends convinced me that I could manage the show. So I finally went to my friend's ward.

"Zahir, mere *bhai*... come here; sit next to me." SG beamed again when he saw me.

I smiled and sat next to him on that same squeaking metal chair.

"Can you please tell me what it is?" he asked pointing towards the ceiling.

'Not again,' I thought. This time I strained my neck to see what else could be there on this roof. After two minutes, I said, "The tube light is reflecting on the cobweb next to the fan," thinking I had covered everything under the roof!

"Useless you are; I'm asking about the lizard. I can't understand how you can miss these things," he grumbled.

"Oh sorry, I didn't see the lizard."

"No problem; do you see that girl sleeping there?" It was a flash back situation, but I had to pretend as if I was hearing this for the first time.

"Ya *dost*, tell me," I asked.

"You know she is my distant relative; both our families fought bitterly over this lizard. Since I claimed to be the owner of this small reptile, she got angry and slept off."

I was at a loss on how to react to such conversations. I just smiled and joined my friends who were consoling his parents.

"*Beta*, how is he behaving now?" his dad asked me.

I looked at them straight and thought I'd better tell the truth. "Uncle, he is not making any sense. He is uttering some gibberish. Don't worry, the doctor has shown a lot of confidence. He said this behaviour is normal with people suffering from amnesia." I tried to convey optimism.

"I don't know *beta*, only you can help us out; you are our only hope," they said in unison.

'Oh god, now why should everyone get emotional?'

"Don't worry uncle, I will take care," I said to comfort the old souls.

We sent them home, took permission from college and planted ourselves in the hospital ward for the next week. His parents brought food thrice a day. For me, it was like having a lavish meal since it was home cooked, and it had been ages since I tasted good home food.

There was not much change in SG; he used to blabber something and I would nod and smile at all his stupid talk. The only relief was the nurse; she would come once every three hours to give some injection. She was my second reason for taking this nanny job. She would walk swaying like a pendulum and flash a flirtatious smile at me.

My friends would juggle between house and hospital. They would always feel jealous whenever I mentioned about that nurse. "Lucky chap, free entertainment and food, and you get to watch TV the whole day," they would say with a heavy heart.

"Come on guys, it's only a matter of days; then I will be relieved of this," I would console them.

A week later, SG was unusually silent and didn't talk too much. At about 6 in the evening, he suddenly sprang up from his bed and said, "Zahir, what are we doing here? Why are we in hospital, and why the hell I am dressed in a patients gown?"

I was so happy that my eyes filled with tears. I hugged him tightly and said, "Welcome back *dost.*"

"Hey, what happened? Why are we here in the hospital? Is anything wrong?" he asked looking very surprised. I just told him to sit for a few minutes and rushed to the doctor.

He examined SG thoroughly, asked his name, parents' names and SG answered sincerely till the point of accident. After that incident, he could not recall anything and had no clue why he had landed at the hospital.

I called his parents and my other two friends. All of them were relieved. As soon as they came, they hugged me and hailed me like a hero. SG was still wondering what this hullabaloo was all about. We explained the entire situation to him and my, my, his face was worth watching. When I recounted to him his conversations during the previous week, he would jump and exclaim, "Did I say that? Oh God," and all us would laugh heartily.

Finally we all in very delighted mood went to SG's house for a dinner", so this is my dear old SG for you he said and burst out into a hearty laugh;it was so loud that many people from neighbouring cubicles stared at us.

Strange they thought, seeing Zahir laugh so much.

Zahir was now in joyful spirits; I could see him smiling and shaking his head.

Sometimes I wonder how strange humans are; we are so dependent on the surroundings to keep ourselves happy or we feel dejected because of the same surroundings. I always believed that if you had a problem, you cannot go searching for solutions in books or talks; you need to get down to the root and solve it.

Anyways, I was relieved that Zahir was no longer pondering on that issue. I had a strange sense of satisfaction, probably experienced when someone is happy because of you.

I just smiled to myself at the thought that philosophy is not a difficult thing; it's only a set of good emotions.

"Will you start your work or laze around?" Zahir commented.

"Oh ya boss... I'll start working," I said resuming my work.

After three hours of sincere working, I went to Zahir

and started talking casually, "So what happened to your *Ghajini* friend?"

"I must thank him for one thing; because of him, we were ab

le to go for a small trip."

"Oh how come?"

"The doctor suggested that an outing would help SG"

Zahir again started narrating an incident to me.

CHAPTER 4
MEMORABLE TRIP

Our class got to know about this and suggested hundreds of places including Haridwar and Tirupathi.

"Why don't you come to my village?" one guy called Shastry suggested.

This was the 'Shastry' of our class, only one of his kind. And he had a liking or affinity towards SG. Shastry was a dim bulb whose boastful ways had created more enemies than friends.

Shastry would always brag about his village; he just wanted a reason to show off his place and found a way.

"Oh that's a good idea; we can stay in his village," SG said turning towards us.

"Oh, hello. Who is that royal 'we'?" Shastry put his hands on his hips and made a face at SG. "I am inviting you and only you to my house, not these Charliezzzzz!" he said looking at us as if we were terrorists ready to attack him.

"I will come if and only if my friends join me, else forget it. We are not begging you for your hospitality," SG remarked.

Having no choice, he obliged, but put forth an exhaustive list of do's and don'ts.

We packed our bags and the next day, all of us left early in the morning. After a pleasant journey, we reached Shimoga, our destination.

It was a small village near Shimoga called Koodli; it was just a sixteen kilometre drive from there.

When we reached there, we saw a palatial house belonging to Shastry's ancestors. 'No wonder Shastry keeps bragging about this,' I thought.

'Shastry Mansion' was written on a huge stone slab outside the house.

The location, which was a hill station, was so beautiful that my friends started taking photographs. The weather was very pleasant and we could feel the freshness of greenery everywhere, small dew drops on the lush green grass, glittering like a diamonds in the sunshine. The place was mind blowing; all of us stood near the gate and admired the beauty around.

Shastry had gone prior to us to inform his folks about our visit.

We opened the gate carelessly; it was a huge iron gate, which had a very old look. The crisp rust near the hinges loosened with every movement of the gate accompanied by a loud creak giving the impression of it being a very old house.

No sooner had we opened the gate that we could hear a faint growl. We froze on the spot. Suddenly from nowhere, this huge animal came bouncing at us, its ears flapping up and down with the speed; none of us had seen this kind of animal before.

"Oh man, oh man, runnnnnnnnn…"someone screamed and all of us took a u-turn to the gate.

While we were trying to save ourselves, PKC was staring at the animal. "Hey, it's a very dangerous dog…" he started.

"Bloody, will you shut up and come out or you want to get killed…" one of us screamed at PKC.

"Hey wait man, I know this breed… it is… it is…"

"You fool, come out," I said dragging him forcibly across the gate and closed it hard, just in time.

Now we could feel its hot breath across the grill; it was barking loudly and our heartbeats were quickening in fear.

"*Oye* PKC, we know you love dogs, but this is no dog; this looks like a malnourished hungry lion. Bloody, you could have got us torn to pieces today, idiot!" Tubbs screamed at him.

"Look guys…"PKC tried to explain, and he was interrupted by a voice, "Junior, hush… silent… good boy… go in…"

The gate was opened by an old man wearing khakhis with a stick in his hand. We presumed him to be the watchman. Before we could say anything, SG shouted at him, "Don't you know how to keep animals tied? What if it had pounced on us? Would you have guaranteed our lives? Useless fellow…"

"Hello young folks, I am Shastry's grandfather," a cheerful voice could be heard, and it was coming from the same old guy in khakhis.

"Oops… I am sorry sir… slip of mind… I mean slip of tongue…"blurted SG.

"Nothing to worry, young man, it happens. Please come in. You are Shastry's college mates right? He told me you guys would be coming by 10; it's only 9 but it's okay, come on in," he said merrily.

We weren't expecting anything like this. We expected an old guy in a *lungi to* be Shastry's grandfather. However, seeing him so fit and fine with a hearty approach, made us feel at ease immediately.

"By the way, this is no animal; he's my friend. His name is Junior and he's a Great Dane," Shastry's grandfather explained to us about that animal as we gathered our luggage and trotted towards the mansion.

The house looked very old but huge, considering only 4 or 5 people stay at any given time. There was a stone fountain at the entrance of the house, which was no more in use and we could see wild lilies covering the small pond, and on either side, there were huge well-maintained gardens and an old man trimming the rose shrubs. A set of pillars covered the portico. There were a few steps to be climbed before entering the main door and an old swing was hanging at the corner.

The door had art work; every nook and corner had figures of elephants, horses and what not. It was about twelve feet high and a lion with a handle was placed right at the centre. We wondered how a door could look that artistic.

When we entered the house we were dumbstruck; the house resembled a palace. A settee was present right at the centre and there was a passage running across the main hall; it reminded us of old *Hindi* movies. There was a carpeted staircase and vases in every possible place, and broad windows with silk curtains; phew! We couldn't stop admiring this house.

Sensing our reactions, Shastry's grandpa started, "This house belonged to my great grandfather; he was a landlord owning 100 acres of land that you might have seen on your way here. Then as civilization grew, we lost almost all our land; only this property was left. This place has been renovated many times though the main pillars are untouched." He looked at us with a sense of pride as if to say that he had preserved the essence of the ancestor's property.

"You guys freshen up ,then we can meet for breakfast. Shastry is on the first floor left side last room. I will send a servant to take your bags."

All five of us were super impressed with this; we went to his room and opened the door.

Shastry was smiling in his sleep. "Definitely thinking about his girlfriend," Tubbs said standing in front of the bed.

PKC asked, "What are you guys planning? I sense something foul."

Tubbs and I looked at each other and gave a notorious smile. Everyone understood.

"Oh... no, no, no... this is his house. You cannot do this."

Before even PKC could stop us or could say anything more...

Tubbs held a water bottle right above his head.

"Wait, wait, wait, damn!... shit," PKC shouted.

Tubbs poured the water on Shastry's face. Within a flash, he screamed .

"Katrina, Katrina, is it raining... what happened..."

Shastry jumped out of bed to see four figures standing in front of him and laughing.

"What the hell are you doing? Shit man; I was in the final moments with Katrina. Idiots, you ruined my climax," Shastry screamed annoyingly.

"What final moments…" Roopak asked with lots of interest.

I interrupted, "Ass, you invited us and here you lay like a buffalo in a murky waters; get up! Show us your house. We have already met your grandfather. You two are as different as chalk and cheese."

"*Arre yaar*," he said rubbing his eye. He was sleeping on such a big cot that it could hold all the five of us. We jumped on the bed and started hitting him.

"Ahh… you rogues… I shouldn't have invited you! Wait, I will call Junior…" The minute he said this, we came back to normal and started pacifying him. This was a thousand times better than that giant chasing us. Meanwhile the servant came with our bags and handed us clean towels and said, "Sir, please be ready within one hour; the breakfast will be served in the common dining room."

We were shown the guest room; it was a huge room with two double cots and a window overlooking the backyard. We could see the fog covered Western Ghats. Even the best of the best resorts can't promise this, I'm sure. We all unpacked, took a bath, got ready by 10.30, and went to Shastry's room. He joined us and all of us went to the dining area.

The dining table was the hugest we had seen till date. It could hold at least sixteen people.

We arrived late. Shastry's parents and grand parents

had already occupied their places and a banana plantain was kept in front of them.

"*Appa, amma, ajji, ajja,* these are my friends, Zahir, Roopak, Tabarez, Sachin and Praveen," he introduced us in a single shot.

"*Namaste* uncle, aunty, ajja, *ajji,*" we sang in chorus.

"Oh ho… hello again boys; please sit down. Liked the place? "Grandpa asked.

"Yes uncle, very nice," we all crooned together.

"So, how are your studies going on? You are aware of the campus interviews right?" asked his dad.

'We came all the way from college to forget that world and here is this bugger asking us about our weak point.' We all looked at each other and could see Shastry feeling odd. "*Appa…*"he started.

Thankfully, the food arrived. Two servants came carrying a big vessel and that saved us.

"Oh here is the breakfast; enjoy dears," said his grandpa.

"Yeah, please feel comfortable and eat," his mother joined in.

The servants served us *idlis* and put *Sāmbhar* and *chutney* on the plantain. We started gobbling up the food the minute it was served. "Ahem… ahem," Shastry coughed forcibly and gestured us to stop eating since there was a custom that elders should start followed by the youngsters.

The family reaction was intimidating. I guess nobody was ever given freedom in this mansion and there were a set of rules to be followed.

"Youngsters have no patience," his father said aloud

looking straight at us. We knew we had done something wrong, so to please them, Tubbs got up from the seat.

"Oh, sorry uncle, shall I serve you water?" he stood up, took the water jug and started to pour. Suddenly the jug slipped from his hand and the entire water splashed on Shastry's father wetting him from head to toe including the floor.

Barely had we recovered from this accident, when one of the servants carrying hot *sāmbhar* slipped and dropped the entire load on Shastry's dad. Unfortunately, his dad was partially bald and the effect of the hot *Sāmbhar* on his pate can only be imagined!

"Sorry uncle… so sorry…"all of us started.

"His father took out a piece of cucumber from his eyes and looked at his mom. She immediately got up and asked one of the servants to fetch the towel.

"Bloody Soma, can't you see and serve?" scolded his grandma.

"Very sorry sir, very sorry, pardon me; the water on the floor…"

"Okay, okay, go inside; don't show your face for another hour."

"Sir, I am sorry… I thought you wanted water…" Tubbs was feeling very bad and his voice started to quiver.

We all looked at each other and controlled our best not to laugh. Shastry's father didn't bother answering and walked out of the dining room. His mom followed, and then his grandma trying to console them.

"Look what you fools have done!" Shastry was annoyed.

"My dad is furious now; he hardly smiles or talks; now thanks to you guys he will not even twitch!"

"Yaar sorry..."

"Ha ha ha ha ha..." Suddenly his granddad started laughing. "You are naughty fellows *haan*. Ha ha ha... he was looking so funny… his poor head!"

That really took a lot of pressure off us; we too burst out laughing; only Shastry was left fuming at us.

We finished our breakfast and his granddad asked us to take a tour of their house, so all of us, along with Shastry, went to discover the place.

He showed us the gardens, the cow sheds and their vegetable garden. We spent half a day going around the house. There was a huge kennel for 'Junior'. He lay on the side and looked at us meanacingly. We just moved away from that place and vowed not to come that way again. We were hungry, so we asked Shastry to get something for us to eat.

"Hey, another ten minutes and lunch will be served," he said.

All of us gathered in the same dining room; this time we were silent and didn't bother to look at his dad.

Luckily the lunch went smoothly. We had an authentic South Indian lunch with *papad* and salads which concluded with a dessert, a sweet dish made out of milk and cream; I don't remember the name but it was good.

After a heavy lunch, everyone went to their respective rooms leaving us and his grand pa. We sat in the verandah, breathing in the mountain air. The hill station was a blessing to us; we never felt so relaxed before.

His grandpa narrated some stories of wild animals he encountered here and how he tackled them. He started recounting all his lifetime achievements and also about his girlfriend whom he loved but had no guts to admit.

"You were in love? That too in those days?" Tubbs was so amused hearing this.

"Yeah, yeah, why not? Am I not a human being?"

"Not like that *ajja*, but …"

"I know what you youngsters think; you feel only you have enjoyed, only you have seen the world; remember we have passed your age to grow old. I can read your minds very well," he smiled.

"We belong to a very strict culture and that came in my way of love. I had no guts to go against my parents and society, so I just decided to marry a girl whom they chose. But my dears, I will tell you, be bold always; say it with all your heart and soul if you love someone. Don't make the same mistake as I did."

'Wish our parents could hear this.'

"Shashi, why don't you take them to our fields?" he told Shastry; they called him Shashi at home.

All of us hit the road. The fields were probably a kilometre or so away. We got a ride in their bullock cart. None of us had seen a real field; we only knew about them from the movies. It was the first time we experienced how it actually felt to be walking on the fields.

There were small canals connecting each field; we started playing in them till someone showed us a snake wading its way through the water. We immediately jumped out thinking it might be poisonous. However, the locals told us that city people had the misconception that all snakes are poisonous. They explained that snakes are more scared than us and they are really helpful for farmers as they keep the rats and rodents at bay.

That day we learnt a lesson; living harmoniously with animals and considering them to be a part of this ecology is what village people believe in and that is something we guys should understand. Here nature is given the utmost priority and in cities it is treated as a hindrance for traffic. At times it pains to see people chopping trees for reasons like, 'branches are coming in the way of telephone wires'.

I don't understand when we people will realize that every tree is a life and we commit thousands of murders every day without being punished. One wonders how long Mother Nature will protect us. I'm sure there will be a day when we will have to pay the devil its due!

We had become thoughtful after visiting the fields and interacting with the locals; we discussed a lot on our way back and decided to do something about this.

It was half past 5 by the time we arrived back. Junior was nowhere in sight which was a relief for us. Grandpa was sitting on the swing and reading. As soon as he saw us, he smiled and beckoned to us.

"Soma, get tea and snacks," he called the servant.

Soon a tray with hot *pakodas* and tea was laid in front of us. We gobbled everything within seconds. Then we started chatting casually about ourselves and our interests. We felt the only person worth talking in that house was his grandpa. The rest were damn serious and showed no signs of entertaining or accepting us. Nevertheless we too showed no signs of disappointment or hesitation since Shastry's granddad was good enough entertainment.

"Tomorrow we are planning to take a trek. Is there any good place nearby?" one of us inquired.

After a lot of discussion, we zeroed in on *Kudremukh*, one of the famous places in Karnataka. It was an hour's drive from our place.

So everything was decided. We sketched a beautiful plan and were excited about it. Shastry's grandpa made all the arrangements for the trip. The only person not willing to go was Tubbs; only god knew why. He continually refused. Finally I put my foot down and said, "You are coming, you have no choice!" The servant interrupted at this point and asked us to come down for dinner.

So all of us walked towards the dining room, but to our dismay, we found that Shastry's father had decided to organize dinner outside in the backyard. It was our chance to arrive at a truce with his dad.

The place was set neatly for ten of us and the moonlight shone brilliantly, and even the food looked delicious.

"We prefer to have dinner outside whenever we come here," his father smiled at us.

We looked at each other and thought it was a very good start.

After a nice dinner, we started walking around. When we reached the cow sheds, Shastry's dad looked at us and asked how many of us had ever tried milking a cow."

We said none of us had tried.

"Would you like to try now?" he asked.

We didn't want to do anything that would upset his dad, so we immediately agreed.

"I will try first," said Shastry's father eagerly. "Soma get *Gowri*." Gowri was the new born calf. To milk a cow, you get the calf to suck the teats of the mother cow and then when the cow begins lactating, you take away the calf. It's heart wrenching when the calf bleats for its mother.

We were looking attentively as if we were born to serve in this field. Tubbs decided to be extra nice and volunteered to take *Gowri*.

"Careful, handle her gently. She is not a dog to be dragged like that." He looked sternly at him.

"No worries uncle, I am good at this," he said as if he has been doing this throughout his life.

After the initial exercise, his dad successfully started milking the cow. Suddenly, Tubbs saw something black moving on the ground; damn! It was a black scorpion. The minute he saw this, he started jumping.

"Scorpion scorpion… uncleee…" and let loose the calf in a frenzy. The minute the calf became free, it sprinted towards its mother, and kicked everything that was in its way. Unfortunately, uncle was also not spared. He too got kicked by that violent calf.

He fell on the scorpion which stung him hard on his left foot… "Ahhhhhhhhhh…" he screamed and held his foot.

Everyone rushed to him, "Somaaaaa… come fast!"

Even 'Junior', who was nowhere in sight till now, started barking. Soma had forgotten to tie him up, so he came charging at all of us. We all started howling and ran hither and thither screaming, "Soma… Soma help…"

Soma was in a fix; he could not decide whether to attend to us or Shastry's dad. He finally thought it better to handle the dog. So he ran behind the dog who was now running behind Tubbs. Finally he caught the dog and dragged it to the kennel.

Tubbs had turned turnip! Everyone gave him a disgusted look. "Shashi what sort of friends you have!" His mother seemed very furious.

"What colour was the scorpion? I have read that scorpions are usually poisonous," PKC started.

All of us banged our hands against our head. 'What is wrong with him,' we thought. The minute PKC said this, Shastry's mother started to cry, "Aiyo Aiyo… poisonous aaaaa…"

Shastry looked worried. "Amma, should I give a will and ask appa to sign just in case…"

"You idiot," his mother said and ran beside her husband.

Now all of us started searching for the scorpion. "If it is black in colour, no problem, but if it's red then dangerous!" PKC said.

We glared at him and said, "Shut up you fool!"

"What wrong did I…"

"Hey there it is… see, see, it's going near that bush… it's… red in colour… oh my God!" SG said alarmed. "That means it's poisonous."

By now Soma and two other servants were taking uncle to his room amid screams and shouts.

"Wait a second; it's a black one." Now the scorpion was clearly visible to us. "It is a whip scorpion; the most common in India and it's not poisonous, so you don't have to worry," I declared.

They looked at me as if I did some miracle. We all rushed to see uncle. Tubbs had not uttered a single word; he just kept his head down.

Finally someone called the doctor; he prescribed some pills and an ointment for the swelling and stated that there was nothing to worry since in these parts, poisonous scorpions were rare.

After this incident, we never left Tubbs alone for a second. We pulled him to the room and dared him to stay put and not move an inch till we returned.

We went downstairs leaving Tubbs locked up in the room. "Aunty, we are sorry…" I said looking at Shastry's mom who was now rubbing the ointment on his leg.

"See what you people have done; in the morning you almost burnt his head and now the calf has kicked him on his right side and the scorpion has bit him on his left side. By now the calf would have finished all the milk. Do you want to take his life or what?" she grumbled and started to whimper.

"Ask her to be grateful that still two hands remain untouched with Tubbs around," PKC whispered slowly to me; everyone sniggered.

"What… what… did you say?"

"Oh nothing aunty… nothing… Tubbs is praying to his Allah in the room."

"Don't take his name!" she said angrily and asked us to go back to the room and leave as early as possible.

We slowly made our way out and wished "Goodnight…" before leaving the room.

"Yeah right… good night after all this."

We went to the room to sleep. Shastry was still angry

with us and surprisingly, even his granddad was nowhere in sight. We were like unwanted guests in their house. The sooner we made our way out the better, we thought.

We all looked at Tubbs and decided that it would be better to avoid the tabooed dining area. We were tired with all this *hungama* and slept peacefully after disturbing the entire house.

The next day we got up early and packed our bags. Shastry's grandpa had already booked the cab which would drop us to a nearby place. The food packs were ready - snacks, water bottles - everything was kept ready for us. Everyone was more than happy about our departure. Shastry's parents didn't speak much and asked Shastry to be careful giving Tubbs a long stare.

CHAPTER 5
LOST AND FOUND

"Guys, please be careful; the land is very slippery and beware, there are lots of leeches," his grandpa cautioned.

"Okay, we will do that," Tubbs said in a low and dejected voice.

The cab dropped us to the foothills of the Kudremukh and went off.

"So now, how we start from here?" PKC asked Shastry.

"Yeah, it is right… no, no… left… ahh, I had come here almost six years back," Shastry said in a very confused state.

"I had vowed not to go for the trek; now see, even this bloody Shastry does not know anything. He was just bluffing in front of the college girls about the trek. Has he even walked a mile on his own? Never! And the way he bragged the other day in front of the girls, stating that he could climb the mountains like a monkey climbing the tree - effortlessly! Bah! I don't know what he is going to take us through." Saying this, Roopak flung a huge stick at Shastry.

"Just shut up, let me think," was all Shastry could say.

"By the time you find out, it will be evening."

There were two young lads walking on the road.

Tubbs suddenly came to life and said, "Shall we hire these guys?"

"Ah, this is the first time in the last one year he has said something worthy and useful," SG mocked at Tubbs.

"Hey, you guys, can you guide us for the trek?" I asked.

"No *Saar*, sorry no trek," said one of them.

"Don't worry, we will pay you for that," I tried to bribe them.

To my surprise, he immediately replied, "Five hundred bucks."

"What bloody, are you taking us to a gold mine or to the falls?"

"*Saar* for two people," he argued.

"No, I will give you only three hundred bucks."

"Okay *saar*, you have to provide the food." We agreed and started the trek.

The trek didn't seem as simple as we thought. We had to look out for the hidden crevices and trenches. I knew that Roopak would burst out of anger anytime. It was almost a ten kilometre one-way trek. I could see Roopak getting tired and irritated.

"*Kaminey*, never ending or what?" Roopak asked Shastry.

"How will I know? It must be eight kilometres or more," Shastry answered.

"Who asked you to act great in front of college girls?" Roopak asked in a clearly irritated voice.

"Don't start it again," I said and we started walking ahead. Roopak and PKC were talking to each other and they were lagging behind. Tubbs was along with us. I was wondering how the trek could be so smooth with Tubbs in our team. I was sure there was something coming in the way.

The two guys who were leading the way were not less than mountain goats. They would easily walk ahead making us look like fools gasping and breathing heavily. We would take so many breaks in between that once or twice they commented, "These folks are best suited for cars and mopeds; they can't do all this," and started laughing.

"Oh this is the way to the falls," I pointed at a shaky wooden board that read 'Hanumangundi Falls'.

As we were going along, "Dham..., Dhoodum..." a sudden sound made us halt in our tracks and we all turned back. "Well guys, no prices for guessing the originator of this sound," I said smiling.

"Of course that bugger; who else can it be?" SG said. Yes it was Tubbs again, without a doubt. He had fallen down. We all started laughing at that sight. "Hey I can sense a land slide; we must warn the villagers," I said still laughing.

We went back to help him. He was a bit fat, oh sorry, too fat, and was unable to carry his own body weight. No wonder he kept on nagging about this trek.

"Hey just check if the earth below has shrunk?" SG said laughing.

"No yaar, due to this impact, another path has been created," I said, showing an adjacent road. At this, all of us, excluding the serious Shastry, started laughing uncontrollably.

"Please show some humanity and help me up," Tubbs said dusting his shirt.

Now our strength was put to test. With all our might, we helped Tubbs to his feet.

"Phew! Achievement man, I say, achievement!" I exclaimed.

Then, we resumed our trek. SG raved about nature and troubled our already troubled ears from Shastry's boring conversation. We had come almost two kilometres ahead of the point where Tubbs had fallen.

"Where is Roopak?" I asked turning back and not finding him.

"He must be dead by now," SG said.

"Where is PKC?" I again asked.

"He must be carrying the dead person," SG again said laughing aloud as if he had cracked the greatest joke in this world.

"On a serious note, where are they? Let us wait for some time," I forced on the other two.

We sat on a rock and waited for nearly 20 minutes but nobody arrived. Now, panic made its way through all of us. At this point those two guys extracted some 300 rupees from us and walked away.

"Where are those two boys going yaar?" SG said looking at the two young guides who were eagerly distributing the cash between themselves.

"Let them go anywhere, what is your problem? I just want to know where those two idiots are," I replied, hoping those two were out of any sort of trouble.

"Oh buggered up man, this useless person." I started hitting Tubbs with the water bottle.

Others were surprised. "Why are you hitting him? He won't get hurt; he is like a thick skinned hippo," SG said giving me a huge stick.

"When we were lifting this hippo, did you guys notice something yellow fallen on the road," I asked suddenly enlightened.

"I think that was the direction board and this huge mass of flesh fell on that and might have changed the direction," I erupted ready to charge at Tubbs again.

"Now, what is my mistake?" Tubbs tried to defend himself.

"So what's new, that is bloody common about him" Shastry said.

"Can't you guys see? What if those two are on the wrong track?" I said.

"Oh shit, now what?" SG sat down putting his hand on the head.

"Someone dead? Why are you guys behaving like this?" Shastry asked.

"Yeah, Roopak and PKC are dead," I said. Tubbs was still scratching his head.

We hurried back towards the road divider and indeed the direction board had changed; we now followed the new path.

"Roopak… PKC…" I shouted at the top of my voice.

I looked at Tubbs angrily. He was least bothered; carelessly he was munching chips sitting under a shady tree. I wished I could be like him, easy going, never bothered about anything.

I heard a faint voice. I got some confidence. I repeated their names, as if I were chanting some mantra. The voice started to grow louder. Then I heard someone abusing Shastry.

It was Roopak shouting angrily on top of his voice.

"I will kill you, man," Roopak said advancing at Shastry with a thorny bunch of sticks. "I told you this fellow will leave us nowhere and we had to hike some four kilometres searching for you guys; you have any idea how the path was?" he showed his half torn pant and PKC was panting like a dog and just kept nodding at what Roopak said.

"We thought you guys have gone ahead and blindly followed the path. After some time we realized that this path was leading us nowhere. Then we started walking back thinking we will just go back to Shastry's house. At that point I heard somebody calling our names. Now why the hell you guys changed the direction? You think it's a joke or something?" Roopak was so furious that his face would have turned red if he was any shade lighter, but with that complexion, we were unsure of the colour of his face presently.

"What should I do if that Tubbs turned the board?" Shastry defended.

"You buggers, you made us go four kilometres extra and that Tubbs is happily eating chips, you irresponsible fools."

"Ah… look, Roopak sir is talking about responsibility; the same person who had lost the neighbour's child six months back, while looking at a call girl in a busy market," I said.

We somehow managed to pacify Roopak and resumed our trek. We had to go down a precipitous slope.

"Whoa… that seems like a deadly slope," I said.

At first it was okay. As we went down, we picked up momentum. Roopak, SG, PKC and I got down the steep block and managed to control our momentum and stop finally.

"Where are Tubbs and Shastry?"

Shastry was still standing at the top and was going to and fro.

Roopak shouted on top of his voice, "What happened, you frightened fool?"

Shastry started laughing. "I pushed Tubbs to go down."

"Where is he? He is alive, right?" PKC asked.

"That fatso lost momentum and dashed into a tree while coming down." Shastry burst out laughing.

"Is he okay?" I asked him.

"I was, in fact, wondering whether the tree he dashed into is okay," Shastry said again laughing at the top of his voice.

"Oh… God damn, Shastry also has a sense of humour. I have never seen him laugh and crack jokes like this."

Suddenly we saw Tubbs shaking his leg vigorously. "Oye earthquake! Run, run…" We all started laughing.

"You creep get out, shoo… go away." Tubbs was looking down at something and was screaming. We all followed his gaze and saw one big fat leech on his ankle. To our surprise, Tubbs had been the only victim of leeches.

"Yeah that is nature's reply," Roopak said teasing him.

"I agree my friend, bloody, he sucks everybody's blood.

Now leeches are taking it out; that's nature," Shastry joined him.

"How did this snake and mongoose become friends?" I asked and saw SG.

He smiled and said, "That's nature."

We took a small paper knife and slid it in between his leg and the leech. Basically we had to remove the sucker, that the leech uses to suck the blood and it required some detailed attention because even if we successfully removed the leech, the suckers can cause infection. It had become one big fat globule, and the minute it fell down, blood started oozing out; it was an ugly sight to watch.

"Tubbs, your blood is going in vain!" PKC said.

"*Yaar* true, it has taken out so much, God, look at that!" Tubbs was still observing the leech.

With so much happening around, we still managed to reach the waterfalls. The falls were about thirty metres high and the water snaked around the rocks and landed down. The place was beautiful; it was worth all the trouble we took. It looked so pure and untouched and the only noises were the birds chirping and the water gushing down.

Without wasting any time, we jumped into the water. It was an amazing experience.

Tubbs was waiting for a chance to avenge Roopak, so he pulled Roopak's only garment inside the water. Roopak got embarrassed in front of everybody and again started blaming Shastry.

Tubbs screamed, "Let's get out for lunch."

"Some more time, *yaar*," PKC pleaded. "This nature

baba will never come out of water," SG said.

We all came out but Roopak was still in the water trying to hide his valuable assets.

We started pulling his leg, and unable to bear it, he swam carefully to the other side, tore a few leaves, joined them together and tied it around his waist.

"Hey, is this called a 'below the belt' joke?"

"Ooh lala la lala lele yo ooh lalala la le lo," SG started imitating a tribal African song. All of us started rolling on the ground with laughter.

Before anyone could catch Roopak, he ran to one corner and started wearing his clothes.

After some more time, we gathered for lunch. We had a heavy lunch. After that, Roopak went to wash his hands near a stone.

"This place looks so very serene, away from human habitation," SG said as Roopak went to wash his hands.

"Oh wait till you see this. Oh man, look at this," Roopak said looking animated.

"What is it?" I asked and walked towards him.

"Come and see for yourself."

"What the hell?" I remarked at the sight.

We saw a hell of a lot of bottles thrown everywhere.

"Phew man, this place is active," I said. "A lot of youngsters might be visiting this place."

"Oye Shastry, look what you have done," said SG pointing towards the heap.

"What man, what you talking about?" he said as if we had uttered something bad.

We all jeered at him and went ahead. Again a thought

came to our minds; people misuse nature so much; not that I'm going to give lectures again, but on a serious note, one wonders where we are heading. At times I wonder why there are travel guides; the more people want to get close to nature, the more they spoil it, including you and I.

Anyways, nothing much can be done; I feel there is no inch left in the world that is untouched; hail the humans!

We started our journey back to Shastry's house for a night's stay. Our return trek was much easier since we were on the right track, but we made Roopak walk in between, just to prevent him from going astray.

Finally we reached the foothill, called a cab and went straight to Shastry's house. There we barely spoke to anyone except his granddad and we crawled to our beds without any delay.

The next day our body ached with all the walking that we had done. Tubbs had it severely; no part of his body was left untouched. He groaned the whole night, "*Aiyo* my leg…"

We decided to have breakfast in our rooms just to avoid any more incidents in Shastry's house. From Soma, we came to know that his father had recovered well and the pain had reduced considerably. This, sort of gave us some relief; we could walk around without any guilt, but still we stuck to the rooms and did not dare to take any risk.

After breakfast, all of us went to meet Shastry's parents. They were sitting in the room chatting. The minute they saw us, their smile vanished like water in a sponge.

"Aunty, uncle, this is for you," we said giving them a neatly wrapped packet.

"What is this?" his mom said showing no signs of emotion.

She opened it and out emerged a sacred thread which we had got from the temple on our way back.

"Aunty this is to protect uncle from any trouble and also for his speedy recovery," Tubbs said.

I think this worked for us; she looked at us lovingly and said, "Thank you dears; it was very thoughtful of you to bring this."

We all beamed with joy when she forgave us; even uncle felt happy and advised Tubbs to develop seriousness in life.

We all took leave and thanked them for their hospitality. We were leaving and Soma just entered the room carrying a bowl of soup.

Tubbs didn't see Soma and dashed against him so badly that the soup bowl flew from the plate and landed on...

"Ahhhhhhhhhhhhhhhh..." Now we didn't even want to see what had happened and ran out as fast as we could.

"Rascals... idiots...." The screams continued from that room.

We finally met Shastry's grandpa .We thanked him and could see his eyes were moist when he bade us farewell; it was emotional.

So finally SG got well, and it was a happy ending," Zahir Zahir ended the story with yet another big smile.

"Oh man, that was good. Nice fun you people had in college," I smiled at Zahir.

"Oh ya, we did; there is more stuff to tell, but madam, do you mind working at least for namesake?" Zahir pointed towards the endless mails which we had received in the past two hours.

"So, story telling over; I should get back to work is it?" I made a long face at Zahir.

"Already you have wasted time; now no more. You are going to stay for two extra hours and compensate for the time wasted," he cautioned me.

Anyways, senior as he was, he could boss over me easily, and at times I really did forget that he was my senior.

So folks back to work; I didn't think he would allow me to talk for another week!

CHAPTER 6
TRAVEL BACK IN TIME

'HAPPY NEW YEAR' read the signs on the office floors; it was the first working day this year, so there were lots of greetings being exchanged.

We three were standing with a *samosa* and chips in our hands. Everyone was enjoying; it was New Year celebrations within our department. Since the management decided not to fund it, we had to organize it ourselves and here we were, standing with the plates and a smile forcibly stuck on our faces.

"*Che*, this is a typical government factory celebration," I declared.

"Yeah, what do you expect? A five star treatment?" remarked Zahir munching those oil-dipped chips.

"You guys enjoy, I will just take an off; celebration or no celebration doesn't matter to me," I said picking up my bag.

"Hey now, now, wait a second; we can have our own celebrations," proposed Zahir.

"What celebration, and where?" asked Vicky still holding the plate with chips.

"Okay, I will select a place…hmm, let's see... How about Rock Café?"

"Okay, it's fine with me and don't ask Vicky, he will just tag along with us," I said.

All of us went to Rock Café, which was about fifteen kilometres from our office. It was well-known for its ambience and also for the service and their eatery, and of course it came at a price!

We reached the place at about 6.30 in the evening. There weren't many people in the café; people had possibly found a better place to celebrate than a café.

It was an old building made up of stones, situated in the suburbs. The walls were covered with dense creepers and in the middle 'ROCK CAFÉ' was engraved distinctly. The look gave me a feeling of an old building.

So, admiring the place, we entered; this was Vicky's and my first visit, but Zahir seemed quite familiar with the place.

"So guys, what a way to start the New Year!" Zahir remarked.

"Yup, impressive," we nodded.

We all placed our orders from whatever we understood in the menu.

After eating, Vicky suggested we play a game of 'Truth or Dare'. We yawned intentionally, but no matter what we did to avoid it he kept on pestering us, so finally we gave up and decided to play.

"Get a bottle bro," Vicky asked one of the attendants.

"Here you go...woo hooo," he spun the bottle and it stopped at Zahir.

"Truth or dare mate!" Vicky said rubbing his hand villainously.

"Dare."

"Propose to her," Vicky said pointing at me.

"Huh," Zahir said.

"What if she is the last remaining woman species on earth," Vicky probed him more.

"I rather remain single throughout my life," Zahir remarked dryly.

"Same here," I smiled back. Both of us started laughing leaving Vicky dumbstruck.

"Buddy, we have known each other for a long time," Zahir responded to Vicky's reaction.

"Loser man," I said and started laughing. "Are you still in your college days or what to give silly dares?"

"Okay, okay… you can see the pink sari that the mannequin is wearing," Vicky said pointing at a sari shop on the opposite side of the road. "Go and wear that sari."

Now that was quite daring; it would take a lot of courage to do that. I looked at Zahir, raising my eyebrows. Vicky sort of raised his collar as if he had thrown a googly at Zahir.

"Okay guys, I choose truth. I'm not gaining anything by that stupid act and moreover, I don't want to disappoint that girl," Zahir said pointing at a couple. We all turned back and looked at them; the girl immediately turned her gaze, and we understood what was happening.

"*Saale*, started again," Vicky said.

"Okay, what do you want to know?"

"Okay, I…" before Vicky could complete his sentence, there was a loud greeting.

"Arre Zahirrrr… how are you *dost?* " The voice boomed over us. A young guy of Zahir's age came to us smiling, and hugged Zahir.

"*Abbe yaar*, where were you? No news, nothing? So happy to see you man," he said excitedly.

"Ah well... I'm fine; how are you?" Zahir said awkwardly.

"By the way, these are my friends-cum-colleagues," he introduced us.

"Hi, I am Roopak," he said and shook his hands with us.

"Oh! so you are Roopak," I said instantly.

He looked puzzled and turned to Zahir. "Yeah, he has told me about you guys," I said reading his mind.

"Oh that's nice; so what all has he said about me?" he asked.

I could see Zahir signalling me and pleading not to open my mouth. "Nothing much; he just mentioned that you were his project mate," I said.

"By the way, what are you doing here alone?" Zahir asked him.

"I was supposed to meet a friend; he just called saying that he won't be able to come. So I'll go back," he said.

"Why don't you join us?" Vicky invited him.

"Yeah, please join us," I said.

"Now, when pretty girls invite me, I can't say no," he said looking flirtatiously at me.

I forced a smile on my face and looked at Zahir. He pretended as if I didn't exist.

"So Zahir, where did you vanish?" he asked.

"You know the reason very well; I just couldn't take it anymore," Zahir said.

"Bloody, it's been seven damn years! We haven't been in touch; you did not miss us? We even called your house but no one answered the calls."

'Bloody' seemed to be their slogan.

"Yeah, we have moved here," Zahir said in a somewhat low voice.

"*Dost,* we searched frantically for you. Can you believe that Shastry was in tears? Man, you didn't feel like meeting us?" he complained.

Zahir just kept quiet and all of us were also silent since this was news to me. I don't know what had happened to Zahir at that moment; he just closed his eyes and sat quietly.

Roopak sensed this was a little awkward and started talking to us. We asked him about his whereabouts and told him what we actually do in our office.

After ten minutes, Zahir said, "Sorry I know it was not good on my part but I was helpless and you knew my situation, right? I was not in a position to take any decision," he said.

"*Arre,* now forget it; I'm happy I met you," he said cheering up. "Anyways you guys are not going out or what?" he asked.

"Nah, we thought of hanging out here. All places are crowded," Vicky said making a face.

The topics seemed to revolve around office or the weather. A long silence masked by forced smiles made us awkward for sometime, and then suddenly Roopak thought of making the conversation delightful.

"Hey wait a second; do you guys know what happened in our New Year celebration? Zahir, you haven't told your buddies?" Roopak suddenly was full of energy and sat upright.

"No, tell us," Vicky said.

"Which one?" Zahir looked confused.

"Fire in the mountain thing!" he chuckled.

"Oh," Zahir said.

"Okay guys, I will tell you what happened on the 31st night eight years ago," he said sounding happy to revive his good old college days.

"Okay, it was 31st night; oh, by the way, I should tell you about the other cartoons in the group. Our group comprised of PKC…"

"PKC, SG, Tubbs and Shastry," I completed the list.

He was perplexed. "Damn man, you must have told her everything; is she your girl friend?" he asked Zahir seriously.

"Yeah, even I keep wondering if these two are going around," Vicky too joined him.

"Shut up guys, sharing stuff doesn't mean boyfriend-girlfriend. THEY CAN BE FRIENDS TOO!" I replied.

"Anyways, I am happy now. I was wondering how could you have such a yumm…ahem … I mean nice girlfriend," he smirked at me.

"Oh, did he mention about our heroics?" He gave Zahir a sly look.

"Now, what do you mean by heroics? Are there some more?" I asked him.

"What do you mean 'some more'? I don't think Zahir has ever studied in college except for monkeying around. If I start telling you guys about him, it will take years!" he said laughing.

"Oh please do tell! We would like to know about our senior," Vicky said.

"Okay, it so happened that we had decided to go out

and party and were not sure where to go. So after a lot of searching, SG located one place. It was on the outskirts of the forest. This place was around ten kilometres from our college. Everyone in our group got agitated with him. We were about to hit him when, "Hey wait, wait... wait till you hear in depth," he jumped back.

"Okay *saale*, what are you going to find in that forest? We should spend our night playing treasure hunt is it?" Tubbs snorted.

"We admit we are party animals, but did you have to take it so seriously?" Zahir asked.

"What do you think we are from Discovery Channel or what to spend our nights in forests looking out for mosquitoes?"

"Or you think we are 'Forest Gump' like you?"

"Will you guys shut up and listen!" SG said throwing his hands up in the air. "I found out that a lot of girls are coming to the party and that is the reason I booked it in advance and now look at the way you guys are behaving."

Now all of us lifted him up in the air and started praising him.

We had three bikes and we were five people, so it took care of the transportation. We all zoomed our way to the forest impatiently. After a lot of searching, we finally reached the place.

"So this is it, guys," SG said showing off as if he had organized the party.

A huge set up was in front of us with 'WELCOME TO THE RAJA'S PARTY' written on a banner. We all looked at SG.

"Isn't that a novel way to write?" SG seemed pleased with the board; we all maintained a dignified silence and looked at each other.

What we saw inside made us feel like thrashing the life out of SG. There was this huge *pandal* that we normally see in village fairs and there were tube lights sticking to the wooden poles and wires hanging everywhere; the music system was like a typical old one with giant sized speakers at the corners and street urchins were there in large numbers.

All of us demanded an explanation from SG.

"Hey, wait! The time they have mentioned is 8'oclock and it's still 7.30; wait till the party gets young," he tried assuring us. "Guys you are forgetting, there will be lots of girls in this party, a very good source has informed me."

"It bloody should be worth 500 bucks," said Tubbs showing his fist.

"Ya, with great difficulty we amassed this amount. I had to tell my parents that my basic clothing is exhausted and it's time I buy new ones," Zahir said making it more difficult for SG.

"Guys, guys, just calm down... I know your young blood is boiling ... just wait... all good things come to people who wait," SG comforted us.

"Oh... welcome, welcome... Please come in..." A man wearing a very dazzling outfit which shone so bright that we had to avert our gaze, welcomed us. To our dismay we saw there was a stage set and colourful lights were being thrown liberally on the stage, multicoloured crepe papers were hanging with balloons and some glitters. It was pathetic; this was too much to digest.

"Sir, when is the party starting?" SG asked him.

"In another ten minutes and please, we have kept some refreshments; you can have them." He showed us the table where a few items looked interesting.

There was a Pepsi bottle with plastic cups neatly kept on one side, and on one tray, there were a few cups filled with Pepsi. Just to worsen the situation, on the next table there was this country liquor being served. There was a large crowd around; some were dressed in bell bottoms and in tight tee shirts.

"This is turning out to be cheap stuff; where on earth you think girls will come?" PKC almost pounced on SG.

Suddenly we could hear a commotion at the entrance. People started whistling. We too were curious and decided to tackle SG later and made our way to the entrance.

Finally the girls had arrived, and it was not even close to our imagination. The party organizers had arranged for dance girls and the band arrived now. Some of its members carried a big banner which read, '*BABY DOLL BAND*'.

Before we could react, the whole crowd erupted and started going near the stage and we were dragged into it by the local mob.

The girls were wearing shimmering skirts with glitters everywhere and a tight top showing off their fat tummies; they had their hair left open and two stars were stuck on either side of their eyes.

The lights were turned off and only the stage was lit.

All the eight girls stood in an inverted V shape with one hand covering the face and the other one pointing up.

"Babuji zaara dheere chalo, Bhijili khadi yahaan bhijili khadi…" crooned the old music player and this song roughly translates to "Oh sir, please walk carefully, I am a live wire…"

The girls started shaking their hips and the crowd started cheering and hooting. Some people even stood on the chairs and danced.

It was the most horrible party we had ever attended. All the four of us caught SG. He started running; Tubbs, PKC, Zahir, myself, all of us started chasing him, for the first time in life. Tubbs was ahead of all of us. He took out his shoes and started throwing at SG.

"Guys… Listen…"

We were in no mood to listen; all we wanted was our money back. He started running towards the other hall where the food was served. Surprisingly even this couldn't stop Tubbs; he was chasing like a mad bull.

We all got tired and started huffing and puffing but Tubbs was still determined to catch him by the neck. SG, not knowing what to do, held a vessel filled with red gravy and swung the contents with full force on Tubbs; we froze on our spot with our mouths hanging open. But little did SG realize that this was like showing a red flag to the mad bull.

Tubbs became more agitated and threw a vessel full of tomato soup on SG. We were still fixed to the ground unable to think or say anything. We started worrying about the mob.

"Somebody should stop them or else we will be killed

by the mob." PKC sounded worried.

By this time, more than half the dishes were on SG and Tubbs and they were looking like a set of buffoons. Tubbs now tried something that nobody could have imagined; he tried to do a somersault by jumping over a table. He looked like a hippo trying to do a high jump. He couldn't even jump two feet, forget about crossing the table. He lost his balance and fell forward on the table. To heat the food, they had placed several small burners. With Tubbs landing on the table, the burner fell on the cloth, and since the cloth already had a share of oil, thanks to these two, it caught fire.

Now the waiters who had gone to see the girls secretly, heard this noise and came back running, but before they could do anything, all the neighbouring tables too caught fire and this spread over the *pandal*.

We got tensed and started screaming their names. Both of them were stunned and were looking at the fire. They realized it was now or never and started running towards us.

"Tubbs, take that speaker on to the right," Zahir screamed.

"Aaa... what... oh, okay..." For Tubbs, it was like plucking a grape from the vine.

"*Jigar ma badi aag hain...*" could be heard from the speaker; 'an irony,' we all thought while running towards our bikes.

"Run fast, *saale*," we screamed at SG.

"Yes... I'm coming. Should I get one more speaker?" he asked.

"First carry your own weight then think about speakers,"

Tubbs said angrily.

There were two guards near the parking; they saw us running and in the background, they could see this huge ball of fire. We were looking like soldiers coming from the battle ground. The whole place was set ablaze and all the people started screaming.

"Guards, please go there; they need your help," PKC said hurriedly to one of the guards.

"*Haan*… what… what has happened…" They started getting tensed.

"Catch them… catch them… that fatso started all this," one of the waiters started screaming.

Tubbs put some gravy on their eyes and pushed them hard; they fell on a set of bikes and since it was arranged in a sequence, they fell one over the other. Luckily for us, we had parked our bikes on the other side.

Zahir and I sat on one bike, Tubbs was behind PKC, and SG had to ride alone.

PKC got so tensed that he started trembling and was unable to start the bike.

"*Saale*, what the hell… start fast," I yelled at them.

"Ya wait…" He was still looking tensed.

Tubbs was restless. "Damn you man, start or else allow me to do it," he growled. By now, the crowd was nearing the parking lot.

"Kick man… fassssst," we screamed at him and drove in full throttle.

"Vrrrooooommmmmmmmm…"Thankfully the bike came to life and he too joined us. All of us drove in full speed as the road was empty.

"Hey, they are following us," Zahir said pointing at the

bike behind us carrying two people - one guard and the other, a waiter.

"Bastards… wait… or else we will complain to the police…" They could be heard swearing at us.

The road was a standard Indian road, which included a lot of humps and bumps. Or, one can say, standard Indian humps and bumps, which included roads in between.

"Dishkquuuan… Dishkquuuan…" Tubbs pretended to carry a gun and pointed at them.

PKC couldn't ride that fast all thanks to the road and Tubbs with that speaker. The guard gathered speed and was very close to them. Zahir was giving me a running commentary of the situation.

"Now, we can see the fielders chasing the ball and the ball is moving forward on a good outfield …" I was wondering how this guy can be this relaxed when the world out there was ready to catch us.

"Oh… narrow miss… the fielders are unable to detect the ball… due to poor light..." The commentary was in full swing.

"Now the bowler tries again and this time the batsman is looking ready and he aims for a sixer but fails." Zahir was referring to Tubbs who was trying to push the bikers away.

"Looks like our batsman is trying to learn break dance."

"Ah… what a shot! Bowled 'em!" Zahir screamed; they had successfully managed to get rid of the bikers. Tubbs finally lifted his leg and pushed them to one side.

All of us now hollered in joy. "Hurray… happy new

year…" We halted at SG's house, thanks to Zahir who had become quite famous there.

The next morning we took the speaker to a local shop and sold it for 1200 rupees. Bloody lost some 1300 in the bargain, but we had turned that place into ashes!

'*Miscreants fire the party hall*' read the local news paper. We saw that and felt proud that we made it to the newspaper headlines.

So this was Zahir and our gang," Roopak said laughing and looked at us.

"Oh my god! Did you guys really do this?" I looked completely astonished. This was more than just an incident. "You guys are really interesting; any document being made on you people?" I asked them.

"Ha ha ha, no, no, not yet…" Zahir was laughing aloud.

"Oh man, we wish we could have some more fun like those days. I still don't get how you could isolate yourself from us," Roopak said suddenly becoming serious.

"I think you know the reason very well; I was unable to handle the pressure any more. The more I am in touch with you guys the more I feel bad," Zahir said.

"So you left without informing them?" I asked wondering how he could stay away from his pals.

"Yeah… I had to…"

"He didn't have to; he got too emotional and later he felt embarrassed to get back," Roopak completed and added, "All because of her!"

We looked at Zahir for an explanation; he just excused himself and walked towards the bar.

"Hey…" I called Zahir.

"No, let him be; he needs some time. I have kindled an old wound." Roopak stopped me.

"Why? What happened? Which girl? "Vicky asked in a single breath.

"Man, it's a long story."

I smiled and said, "From the time we have met Zahir, we have been listening to his stories and we enjoy them a lot, so I am sure this too will be one of its kinds."

"Yeah, yeah that too a girl; I was about to ask him the same question about girls and you joined us," Vicky said.

"Can we talk about something interesting?" Roopak said and then, turning towards me said,, "So what kind of a girl are you? Silent or talkative types? Actually I shouldn't be asking this question to a girl right?" he said cheekily.

Vicky was staring at us like an owl. "Ahem… So Vicky, tell us about yourself." Roopak suddenly changed the topic sensing his long stare.

"You first tell us about the girl." Vicky was adamant to know.

"Well… she is very beautiful and if I get to know her then I will tell you," he said winking at me.

"That means you don't know her? Haven't you met her?" Vicky asked surprised.

"I am with her, and I'm sure as time passes, we will know each other very well, right?" Roopak said not taking his eyes away from me.

"What! Have you already married her? Zahir knows about this?"

"What married? What are you talking?"

"You said you are with her."

"Yes, I said I am with her, but I did not say anything about marriage."

"Oh… you are in a 'live in' relation"?"

"What nonsense; if I really like her then I will marry her. Why should I get into this kind of arrangement?"

"Then you don't love her?"

"That I don't know; it's just the first day," he said touching my half filled glass with his.

"Oh, she shifted yesterday to your place?"

"What shifted? She is still here."

"Here, you mean in this café?"

"Don't behave like a jerk, she is sitting with us!"

"What? Where, I can't see her? Oh my god, she is dead? And, and, and, you can see ghosts?"

"What ghost? What are you talking about? Can't you see her?" Roopak said pointing at me.

"Omigosh! So you lied to me; you and Zahir are old time lovers! How could you do this to him?" Vicky was looking at me in disbelief.

"What old time lovers? What are you talking about?" I said.

"Don't pretend; I know your secret now, all thanks to Roopak."

"What is happening here?" I said looking totally confused.

"Now when did I say Zahir loved her?" Roopak too had a confused look.

"Just now you said that she is very beautiful, she is here with us right now, blah blah blah…"

"Yeah I was talking about her," he said pointing at me.

"Oh, weren't you talking about Zahir's girl friend?"

Both of us banged our heads against our fist.

"Gee… I am sorry, I thought…" Vicky gave a sheepish smile.

I flung the empty bottle at him. "Stupid, how can you think like that?"

"Hey sorry, sorry… Roopak continue yaar…"

"Now if the confusion is over, I will proceed with Zahir's story," Roopak said.

"Yeah that's better, please start," Vicky and I said.

"All this started with the youth festival that took place in the fourth semester; there was a girl called Rashmi and he had gradually developed some liking towards her right from day one. And in the sixth semester, it took a new turn. I think it's better if Zahir shares it with you guys rather than me narrating it."

"Oh that sounds good. Let's call him here," I said going towards the bar counter where Zahir was sitting. Somehow I managed to pull him to the table and we forced him to share his story.

"I really don't want to talk about that. It's past and let it be there. I don't want to revive those incidents again," Zahir protested.

But Roopak finally convinced him to start, and with reluctance, he started.

CHAPTER 7
LOVE 'ISSTORY'

I was sitting in the college canteen and waiting for Rashmi.

"I won! Yes, your treat," someone screamed in joy and hit me on the back.

"What did you win?" I asked looking baffled.

"*Arre*, I told you na, Shri and Arun are going around. You didn't believe me that day; now I have proof that they are together," she beamed.

"Oh... that... I almost forgot..." I said, wondering how girls remember this stuff.

"Well you know Priyanka? The one who wears heavy make-up? Her friend's common friend is Shri's sister and she has heard them get mushy over the phone," Rashmi said as if she had achieved something great.

'I really don't get these girls, man! Just to prove someone's affair, they go on and on! I wish the same effort was put when they solve math questions.'

"Okay, you won! Happy? So what do you want?"

"Hmmm... I like that café which has a balloon floating on the top; let's go there," she crooned like a kid.

"So deal! Let's meet at five today." We took our bags

and headed back to class.

"Are we ordering something or just looking at each other?" Rashmi put the menu down hard on the table later in the evening when we reached the café and had settled down in our seats for nearly ten minutes.

"Oh sorry, I mean… I almost forgot… I normally forget things when I see you." I scratched my head.

I went to the counter and forgot to ask her what she wanted to have and so I shouted, "What would you like to have?"

She made signs about some coffee in the menu.

'That will get over in minutes,' I thought.

"Boss, give me something that will last for a long time," I said winking at the attendant.

"We have a drink sir, it's called cold crushers, which is a blend of cream, rich coffee…"

"Boss, I don't care even if you have some stones in them; just tell me how long it will last," I asked impatiently to the attendant.

"Half an hour and since it's a girl, I can say 45 minutes confidently sir!" he said smiling at me and handed that 'whatever-crusher' to me.

I went over to the table and said, "They suggested this drink, just try this," and gave it to her.

"I have never seen you with any of the boys, I mean… having a cup of coffee… or interacting with them…" I started the conversation to break the silence between us.

"No I prefer being to myself" she said, after which our conversation was limited to our studies , our exams and so on. Though I was not very keen to talk about this, had no choice, talking to her was my main motive, where the conversation was headed was not of my concern. We came out of the cafe' only to see my friends standing at the entrance.

"Hi Zahir, how come here? We thought you had some important work," PKC said sounding very serious.

"Um… well… I had some time you see… so…" I replied.

"Hi guys, how come here?" Rashmi smiled at my friends.

"Oh we came for some quick coffee," SG said.

"Quick? I almost took an hour to finish mine," Rashmi grumbled.

They all looked at me "Well… it's a new drink… and they said it's good, so I got it for her…" I said looking at those wide eyes.

"Oh is it? We should also try it once. By the way, how is this project shaping up?" Tubbs asked pointing indirectly at Rashmi.

"What is he talking about?" she inquired raising her eyebrows.

"Nothing, just about the project we are doing." I tried to cover it up.

"What project? There is no project work for us this year," Rashmi said still wondering.

"I mean… Is it…? What are you talking useless fellow!" I shouted back at Tubbs pretending to know nothing.

"Oh really? We thought you guys are working on some project, right PKC?" Tubbs teased.

'Oh man, why does he do this?' I put my hand on my head.

"Guys, guys, if we do a project, we will put it up on the notice board okay!" I showed my fist at them and pulled Rashmi to drop her off to her house.

"You guys are funny," she said sitting behind me. Honestly I couldn't hear a word; her aroma was making me dizzy and I was a little intoxicated with that smell and the entire way I was thinking about those lovely lips and…

"Hey stop, stop; my house is close by; I will go on my own from here," Rashmi said putting a hand on my shoulder.

Man it was like a 1000 volt or maybe 11000 volt shock to me!

"Oh sorry…" I said. She got down and said 'bye'. I was still thinking about the hand and with a sigh, I went back to my room.

"It is a historic day for this college," our HOD said the next morning. "We have got to host the youth festival this year and it is a very great event as you all know."

I asked eagerly before he could finish, "Which department is given the responsibility of hosting this festival?"

"Unfortunately it's not our department," his voice dropped.

"Oh shucks, we are the best equipped lot to handle large scale events, sir!" Harish stood up.

"That is the only thing we are good at." Shirish poked in between.

"The principal did give a thought about this, but he insisted on others. He said they too should be given a chance. We have a final discussion in another ten minutes. I'll try to convince him," he said with a wink and left.

After an hour or so, our HOD came back and announced, "We are the chosen one!"

"Please keep quiet; please don't scream." Nobody was listening to the HOD; everyone was in a mood to celebrate.

"We will be hosting this festival along with the bio-medical department. I insisted on involving the bio-med department," he said with a smile which was an odd indication from HOD.

"Wow…" Again everybody started screaming, because the bio-med girls would be involved in the youth festival.

"Okay, we have only one month for hosting this festival," he said his voice turning serious.

"No, that's not possible, sir, we have internals in between," I stood up and complained.

"Don't worry about the internals; I have talked to the principal and he has agreed to give us an extension."

This festival is for uniting all the other colleges; we call them over, have some shows and competitions including group discussions, debate competitions, collage works and all sorts of games. So basically it's party time, and only a few privileged colleges can host it. We were proud that our college was considered among them.

Soon the day arrived and we had organized a neat skit from a very famous movie. And Rashmi was given a prominent role to play. She was supposed to enact the role of 'Chandramukhi' in the famous show 'Devdas'.

The story went like this… a rich man took his ailing heart

to a courtesan to help him forget his love. However, he was loved by the courtesan. The moral of the story is that love can destroy and can change one's life. Here, 'Chandramukhi' (Rashmi) was the courtesan.

The curtains began to unroll and Rashmi was standing near the door wearing a bottle green *Anarkali* dress with heavy embroidery work.

The play started.

"*Dev Babu...*" She stretched her tender arms beckoning the guy.

"Oye, Chandramukhi, what's your rate?" A boy from a different college started teasing as if he was checking out a call girl. There were four more boys with him and all of them started laughing raucously.

Roopak was one of the organizers and he was assigned to take care of this show.

"Excuse me, please be quiet." Roopak asked the boys not to shout.

"Any problem dude?" the boys replied and they seemed to be drowned in booze.

"I request you not to shout and tease anybody," Roopak again pleaded them.

"Chandramukhi, we will become Dev Babu for you." they started teasing again and this was loud enough to be heard in the entire hall.

Before Roopak could butt in, he was pushed hard. He got a handful from those five guys.

"What the hell has happened to you?" I asked. I had just entered the hall to see the play.

"Those guys",Roopak pointed at the five guys who looked completely sloshed,"They are from the rival college, and were teasing Rashmi."

"Then what happened?" I asked, livid.

"I tried to stop them, but they did not listen to me; they pushed me and started beating me," Roopak said and his eyes were swollen badly because of the brawl.

"Nothing happened to Rashmi right?" I asked him.

"No, she was on the stage."

"Where is that fatso, Tubbs? PKC? SG?" I enquired.

"They are hosting the show," Roopak said.

"Call them and come to the ground."

"Hey you guys, come over to the ground; we will tell you what the price is," I shouted across the hall to those five guys.

We all gathered behind the ground.

"What happened? Are you giving us a treat?" Tubbs asked breathlessly.

"Those guys were teasing Rashmi." Roopak pointed at the guys.

"These people were teasing our *bhabhi?*" SG was so ready to fight with them.

"Let's go and teach them a lesson," I said.

"Here in such a crowd? It will disrupt everything." PKC, as usual, with his cautious approach tried to stop us.

"You rouges!!"Tubbs screamed and charged at those guys. He hit them with such force that all the five fell one over the other like a pack of cards.

Seeing this, the other guys tried to handle Tubbs with great difficulty.

"Let's go," I screamed.

"Hit him, hit him," Roopak said in full revenge.

We beat them black and blue. Before we could realize,

we had disrupted the whole function. The chairs were scattered here and there. The food was spilled everywhere. The entire place was such a mess. A crowd had gathered around us.

"What the hell have you done? You are supposed to be the organizers of this show," one of the professors butted in and yanked Roopak hard, who was pounding one of those guys with his fist.

"Sir these people were creating a nuisance," I interrupted.

"You shut up. I know you; you are the guy from the chemical department Right?" he said as if my hoardings were put everywhere in the college.

I was surprised that he knew my name. Meanwhile, all of us made a beeline to the principal's chamber.

Rashmi was standing back and looking at me in a disgusted manner. Everyone was thinking that I had spoiled the program and I was the culprit.

"These guys spoiled the whole show on the college ground." The professor showed us in front of the principal as if he was showing a herd of cows greedily making their way to his fields.

"Okay, you can leave Mr. Jayram, thank you," the principal said crisply, which reflected unassuming confidence.

"You are Zahir right? The very popular guy in the college," he said looking at me with those penetrating eyes. Bloody I had become so famous in such a short period?

"Yes sir," I said looking down, to avoid making eye contact with him.

"I was like you in my college days," he said, to our surprise.

I again answered, "Yes sir." Everybody was looking at me perplexed, wondering what was transpiring.

"So, I don't want to hear any nonsense other than the truth. I want you to explain the whole thing, Zahir," he said looking at me.

I explained to him the whole story.

"Not very convincing," he said.

"Sir, what would you do if a miscreant eve-teases your wife?"

I put a confident face and spoke to him straight. Everyone signalled to me to keep quiet, but I was in no mood to listen to anyone.

"We tried to explain to those people, but they became ruthless and started beating Roopak. And they were teasing the girls on the stage," I said pulling Roopak in front of him and showing the bruises. "Sir, one more blow and this guy would have left this world for good," I said intensifying the situation.

"Now you see sir, this incident will give a clear indication that nobody can mess with our college and get away easily," I said raising my voice.

"What about the reputation of our college" the principal asked.

"Sir we owe an apology to the people and we will personally give a letter to the attending heads of the colleges. We will do that sir," I replied.

"I knew that you had something in you; I am very proud of you guys, but no more fights," he said and relieved us.

All of us were astonished that we were not punished; in fact we were praised. On our way back, the entire college was standing near the ground and all of them looked at us as if we were some smugglers caught in the act. And the look on Rashmi's face showed her disgust for me.

"Hey, here you are," I said.

She moved away, my voice falling into deaf ears.

"What is the matter? Why are you running away from me?" I asked.

"I don't want to talk to you, just get lost. I don't want to see your face. You have completely spoilt the show," she said crossly.

"I can explain."

"No need, I know wherever you are, this is bound to happen."

"Will you listen to me!" I pulled her back holding her wrist tightly.

She struggled to pull it back, but I held on. I pulled her behind the pillar and went close to her face. Looking deep into her eyes I said, "I did this because of you, got it? Those guys were passing some lewd comments about you! I couldn't stand it!"

Before she could speak, I went off feeling dejected. I thought that this was the end of my relationship with Rashmi..

She tried calling me but I didn't turn around and stormed away.

I just asked Roopak to make sure Rashmi was safe and headed straight to my room.

CHAPTER 8
GO GOA!

The next day, I arrived early and went to the main auditorium. I was supposed to host a game show. Since I was way too early, nobody had come. I sat on the stage alone lost in thoughts, when suddenly something sharp prodded my back.

I turned to see white sleek sandals. A voice as sweet as honey asked me, "Hello, will you join me for a cup of coffee?"

"Hey, what a pleasant surprise!" I said as soon as I saw her. She was my cousin Rukhsana who was staying in Mumbai.

"I had come to visit *chacha* and he said some function is going on in your college, so I dropped my luggage at his place and took a rickshaw," she said.

"But….but… how could you locate me?" I asked her.

"Oh, there is a board outside giving details of all the events and their venue including the hosts. I just followed it and here you are," she said smartly.

"Are you joining our college by any chance?" I teased her.

"No way, I like my medical stuff very much," she said

with an air of a typical medical student, hinting that engineering was nowhere near her interests.

"What do you know about engineers? We are the ones behind all the tools and everything in the world moves because of engineers!" I pulled her ear and showed her the fan rotating above me.

"If people are alive, then they can think!" she gave a tough fight.

"Dear, these are never ending fights, forget them and tell me how you turned so beautiful; you were such an ugly duckling!"

"That was three years back! Now I have changed," she said haughtily.

She was wearing a blue *kameez* that showed her full figure .She was my distant cousin and my mom had suggested my name to her mother for marriage in another four years. Now looking at her I thought, mom's choice is good at times.

"What happened to you? Why are you sporting a beard? Want to become a *mullah* or what?"

She too looked cute when she smiled. Now why do girls look cute when they smile? And more importantly, why do all girls look cute when they smile? Don't ask me!

"Nah, got tied up organizing this event," I said.

I looked at my watch; my event was about to start in another half an hour. Just then Roopak, PKC and Tubbs came in. I introduced my cousin to them and requested them to take care of her.

"Look, my event is about to start. Just stay with these guys, I will join you once this gets over," I said and went for the preparations.

"Okay, let's go and have something; I am very hungry..." Rukhsana said as soon as I wrapped up the event.

We went to the canteen and ordered some food. I was getting her food when I saw Rashmi glaring at me furiously.

"Hi..." My words fell flat, as she walked away and sat in another corner with her friends.

"Who's that girl" Ruks asked (I called her Ruks at times).

"Yeah, she is my class mate," I said.

Ruks interrupted, "Anyways, tell me how's life. How are your studies going on?"

"Life is fine *yaar*. It's good. I like it here - people, food, college, campus - everything is nice. Ask me about anything except studies." I grinned at her munching on *papad.*

"How about your life?" I inquired.

"Oh, mine is great; we have to read a lot," she said, searching for the onions on her plate.

"Are you dating anyone or still romancing the bones and skull?" I said recollecting my roommates doing something with a skull last year.

"Ah, that's interesting, and better than guys!" she said making a face.

She was really pretty, but every time I thought about her, Rashmi's face would surface in front of me and I would think no girl was a match for her.

"Please take me to the dance competition you are having in the afternoon," she said after we finished eating.

I tried to look for Rashmi, but she had already left. It was more than a day since I had spoken to her and this was pinching my heart.

"Can we go?" Ruks interrupted my thoughts.

"Okay, no problems," I said.

I took her to the dance competition. I made her feel comfortable and asked my friend Priya to take care of her and left for other work.

"Who is that girl?" Rashmi demanded, hands on her waist, as soon as she spotted me.

"She is my distant cousin Rukhsana, why? What is the problem?"I replied happy to see her.

"Oh… so busy that you didn't even look at me while having food!"

"I was searching for you, but I couldn't find you anywhere," I tried to convince her.

"Yeah, yeah, only if you get some time of her pretty face you will look at others na," she snapped.

"*Arre yaar* listen to me…"

"Oh, that too a pretty Muslim girl. Not bad, you have made a good choice," she said not listening to me and dropped her bag heavily on my leg.

"Hey… wait," I said.

She lifted her bag and stormed away pretending not to hear.

'Man, my leg, dunno what was in her bag! I can never understand these girls. They are like… forget about it,' I blabbered to myself and went on to host my next show.

Rashmi and I were supposed to host this show together, so I was really excited and looking forward to conduct this.

After introducing the event and its terms, both of us had to go back stage while the performance was on. It was a song competition so we had nothing much to do other than to announce the names of the participants.

I kept staring at her and she, at times, would straighten her hair, play with the pen, and when our eyes met, she would shy away immediately. Suddenly, I winked at her, and she looked at me horrified as if I had done something wrong! I could see that she felt very shy and bent her head.

Oh man how I loved it!

"What did you do?" she asked when the show was over.

"Me? I was hosting the show." I pretended as if I had done nothing.

"No, no, when you were not hosting the show, behind the curtains."

"I was thinking about the next event."

"I saw you wink!"

"Yeah, natural behaviour, when I saw that beautiful girl performing on the stage."

"But… I thought…"

"Yeah what did you think? Are you, by any chance, saying you mistook that the compliment was for you?"

I had crossed my arms and was looking down at the 5.4 feet homo sapien who had stolen my heart.

"Okay," she said and was about to exit when I put my fingers in my mouth and whistled loudly and winked at her.

She gave arguably the cutest smile I had ever seen in this world and left the hall.

I was so joyous that I almost forgot Ruks was still with me, so I ran to the dance show.

"Hi, how was the show?" I asked.

"Man, engineering colleges rock. I never thought you have so much of fun." She looked pleased with the dance show.

"This is nothing; why don't you join our college?" I said smiling at her.

"Nay, I am okay with my medical. Okay then, its quite late; uncle must be waiting for me."

I looked at my watch and it was half past 7.

"How will you go back home?" I asked her.

"I will take a rickshaw," she said confidently.

"No wait, it's too late; it's better I drop you. Just wait for a minute here. I will just inform my friends to take care of my part of the work."

We went on the bike and I dropped her at my uncle's house.

"Come in," she forced me.

"I can't; I have some more work to be done. My friends and professors will be waiting," I tried to resist.

"I want to tell you something," she said meekly.

"Yeah, tell me," I said looking at my watch and worrying about Rashmi.

"I honestly dunno how to start; I think it's better you come in," she said looking at me differently.

"Okay," I said and followed her inside. My uncle had left a note saying he will be late. Since nobody else was at home, I felt bad leaving her alone so I thought I would wait for some time.

Meanwhile I made a call to Roopak and was relieved to find that Rashmi had already left with her friends.

So I eased a bit and started chatting with her. In between the conversation, she suddenly became silent and said, "I have to ask you something."

"Yeah, please go on."

"Do you love anyone?"

"Well… why do you ask?" I said wondering if she had seen me flirting with Rashmi.

"I…I… look Zahir, from the time *ammi* suggested your name for marriage, I had a special corner for you. I know it's too early for both of us, but take your time and tell me."

The question came out of blue and I was taken aback.

"Ahem…" I said clearing my throat. "Rukhsana, you are a nice girl, but… but… I mean… I haven't thought about… you know what I am trying to say right?"

We were silent for almost five minutes. I could see the dejection on her face. Although she was trying to pretend that she was fine, I knew I had let her down.

"Ruks… please try and understand…"

"I know Zahir, it's completely okay. I respect your decision," she said holding back her tears.

At that moment, my uncle called and said he would be home in another ten minutes; so I thought I'd better leave.

"Look, I am very sorry I hurt…"

"Shhh… don't say anything; I will cry, it's okay," she said turning her back towards me.

Having nothing much to say or do, I just apologized and left; I could see her cry.

I started my *gadi* and went back feeling bad for what just happened.

Next day, I called Rukhsana and found out that she had already left, so having nothing much to do, I joined my friends.

The fest ended in high spirits.

The classes resumed back to normal, but things between me and Rashmi didn't improve.

After the internals, our HOD had good news for all of us. He had organized an industrial trip to G-O-A! This was the result of our hard work for the youth festival. I forgot to mention that we had bagged second place for the event.

I felt this was my chance to get close to Rashmi. I was literally going mad staying away from her for so many days.

Finally the D-day arrived and all of us packed our bags and got into an old *khatara* bus. It was 9'o clock at night. After all the arrangements, we left our college by 10 pm. It was a 4-5 hour journey but due to some confusion, we ended up travelling at night.

We all started howling as soon as the bus started and left people on the streets wondering if this bus was directed towards the asylum.

I was forced to occupy the last seat and again missed a chance to sit with Rashmi.

"*Yaar*, I wanted to sit in the middle row," I complained to PKC.

"Oh please, as if she would allow you to come near her after all this," SG said starting his iPod.

"*Saale*, you don't have a proper underwear, using an iPod and all!" Tubbs leaned back and snatched the iPod.

"Oye, *saand*, careful; I have got it from my neighbour," SG said grabbing his iPod back from Tubbs.

I craned my neck to see if Rashmi would turn. "Even

if you sing or dance, she won't turn! Come back and enjoy!" SG said and pulled me back to the seat.

True, neither did she give side glances nor that sweet smile.

"Okay guys, let's play *antakshari*," Tubbs said suddenly getting up.

"Oh please, let's not become typical. Think of something else," I suggested, and after a lot of brain storming, we came up with the idea to play 'passing the pillow'. Since a pillow was not available, we decided to use a cap.

"Why don't we use Roopak instead of this cap?" SG suggested and started laughing.

"Yeah right! Why not use SG's disintegrated brain?" Roopak gave back to SG.

"Does he have one?" Tubbs said and again creating more laughter.

"Okay, the rules go like this; we play music and start passing this cap, and after sometime, I will stop the music. Whoever has this cap will have to do a task," Sudendra, one of our batchmates announced, and started the music player next to the driver's seat.

"*Koi kahe kehta rahe…*" the old recorder started singing.

"Oye pass pass…" Finally when the music stopped, Tubbs was holding the cap.

"Aha, I was waiting for this," Roopak said rubbing his hands. "*Mote*, you are dead now!"

"Dear girls and boys and lecturers, we are happy to present a great dancer in front of you today. So please, put your chappals together… oops, I mean please put your hands together and welcome Tubbs!"

Lights, music and action! Tubbs stood in front of the

bus. The whole crowd in the bus was excited.

He stood sheepishly in front not able to do anything.

"You talk so big about my brains; now shake your gorgeous body!" Roopak said adding fuel to the fire.

After a lot of hesitation, Tubbs lifted both his hands and started performing the snake dance. This was the task given to him. And the best part was , he had to sing and dance to his own tune.

"Teene nee ne nee ne ne…" He feebly started singing and started moving like a snake.

"Guys, guys, see the Anaconda do a belly dance," someone said in the crowd. It was truly a funny sight; a huge mammoth sized creature trying to be graceful.

Hari, one of our classmates, who was sitting in the front row, started behaving like a snake charmer. A few guys whistled, trying to encourage him. Thanks to the Indian roads, Tubbs didn't have to put too much effort to shake.

"If he continues this item number, the bus will lose its balance," Ganesh said clapping his thigh. This time, the bus driver too couldn't control; he also burst out laughing and the helper stood near the door to control his giggles.

"Guys…ah… ah… enough…hhh," Tubbs said.

"No way! If you stop dancing, we will have to display your collection of pictures of roses," Roopak said gesturing towards Rosy, Tubbs' secret crush!

Hearing this, Tubbs started dancing more vigorously, and at the same time, the bus jerked forward because of a huge pothole. Tubbs lost his balance and fell in front. Laxmi Swamy, a very traditional and reserved girl, had occupied that place. She spoke to none in the class, not even girls. 'Too modern' or 'shameless' were the only two words she used to describe the girls and we guys turned out to be mere dung beetles. Tubbs fell directly on her; there was a huge uproar because of this. All of us nearly fell from our seats looking at this.

She slapped Tubbs hard and with great difficulty, two guys lifted him up. We all checked if she was still alive or crushed. Luckily she had moved aside and Tubbs had fallen on her left hand.

She gave him a mouthful and was about to cry when Rashmi stepped in and consoled her.

After this commotion, the lecturer who was controlling his anger all this while, got up and asked us to watch our behaviour and stopped our game.

"Useless idiots, get back to your place I say," he said looking at Tubbs. He nodded obediently and walked back, this time maintaining his balance to avoid further repercussions.

But we couldn't control our laughter and as soon as Tubbs joined us, we all started laughing again. He was so angry with us that he looked ready to kill us.

We asked the professor's permission to switch on the TV; he flatly refused. After a lot of promising and pleading, he gave us half an hour of viewing. Some people had brought a few DVDs of horror movies, which we thought of playing.

"Oye, Hari, go play this." Roopak gave one DVD from his bag. Hari took it and inserted the DVD into the player and pressed the 'play' button. The whole crowd became silent when the TV came to life.

Roopak turned towards me and said, "*Yaar*, this is THE EXORCIST movie, damn scary. I want that Baby Kutty to die watching the first scene." 'Kutty' was the name of the professor; he was a Mallu Christian. We all praised Roopak for this and with our feet on the next seat, we settled down to watch the movie munching on chips.

A beautiful hand was shown filling a glass of wine. "Hey is this how the movie starts?" SG asked looking confused. "I don't think…" We suddenly realised what was happening and looked at each other.

Kutty had caught a glimpse of what was on the TV.

"Nothing sir… it's a commercial," I said now holding my hand up and completely blocking the view. By then we switched off the TV and the screen went blank. Somehow I convinced him and came back to my seat; all the girls looked at us in disgust. We apologized and silently came back to our seats.

"You knuckle head, what the hell is wrong with you?" I asked Roopak.

"Well… sorry *yaar*… I … think I gave you the wrong one," replied Roopak with a confused look on his face.

"Presence of mind Zahir!" Tubbs said patting my back. I simply nodded and occupied my seat. After this incident, the crowd had hushed down; the only noises were from the girls' bangles and Tubbs snoring at the top of his voice. The five-hour journey turned out to be a seven-hour journey due to the old model *khatara* bus!

CHAPTER 9
DEEPLY MADLY DO

"Good morning sir, how are you?" SG went and greeted the professor, who was busy looking at the travel guide.

"Fine, good morning to you too," he said not looking up.

"Sir, what are you reading?"

"Travel guide."

"Sir, what is written?" SG had vowed to irritate this professor.

"It's about Goa!"

"Sir... what is written?" SG asked again.

Unable to bear him any longer, the professor stood up and started reading aloud so that the entire crowd could hear.

"For an average tourist interested in having a good time, Goa is the ideal place to visit. It is all about beaches..."

"...and babes," PKC said aloud.

The prof ignored him and continued, "...and has one of the finest stretches of sandy coastline and the main item..."

"... sexy *chikni angrez* girls, having a sun bath," PKC

interrupted again; this time he received a whistle or two for the comment.

The professor understood our motives and gave a hard stare at us. We looked at him innocently as if nothing had happened.

"Sir, that's it?" SG probed more.

He glared at SG but to our surprise he continued, "… Having been ruled by colonial Portuguese for over 410 years, one can still find a distinct Portuguese flavour or what-you-call, the traces. This becomes apparent once you hit the Goan borders…"

"… now who cares who came, who ruled, I am more concerned with who comes now? And what they wear!" PKC interrupted again. And all the guys said, "Wah, wah…" for all these one liners!

"You guys have lost all the shame in life! Don't you know what to talk and what not?" Saying this, the professor threw the guide book and slumped angrily on his seat.

It was wee hours of morning and we decided not to trouble him more and spoil the entire day. We reached Goa. We were given a bungalow converted into a hotel, which was situated on a shore.

The guys occupied the top floor which had about eight rooms and the girls occupied the ground floor.

My friends and I took the last room facing the sea. "Nice room," I said opening the window and letting the cool breeze in. it was early morning - 6'o clock - so the sun was still on the horizon and the hues of the rising sun had a brilliant effect on the water. Immediately, we took our cameras and caught it.

We went around checking other rooms. After freshening up, all of us met for breakfast which was served on the top. I tried to make some eye contact with Rashmi but she was too busy looking at her plate. So I too didn't bother.

We then took our bus and went to the industry to start off our so-called industrial tour. It was a fertilizer industry.

"*Arre* Tubbs industry!" someone from the group screamed.

Everyone looked at the name and started making fun of Tubbs. "Gobar industry!" PKC called out loud to Tubbs.

"You guys have no idea about the goodness of Gobar!" Tubbs snapped back at PKC.

After touring the fertilizer industry, we returned to our hotel, famished and tired. We went to our rooms to take a good shower and joined the others for dinner.

We ate in complete silence and came back to our rooms and hit the bed. The first day was very dull and nobody had the energy for some fun.

The next day, we were supposed to visit a pharmacy industry. Due to some problem, they asked us to delay our visiting time. So all of us sat in our rooms and tried to kill time.

Some boys went out on the pretext of shopping. They came back carrying huge bags and dashed to their rooms. We all gathered to see what they had shopped and undoubtedly there were many bottles of drinks, some local and some branded. Since Goa is a paradise for hot drinks, these guys had got them in bulk.

We then had to rush out immediately to prevent the professor from suspecting us. We all went and sat in the waiting room whilst the girls moved in and around the beach for some shopping.

Tubbs and SG too had joined the girls - not our classmates, but the hippie girls. They had befriended two *goris* who had come from Australia. They were wearing a sarong around their waists. God knows what they found so interesting in Tubbs, because all the four were in deep conversation and we could see Tubbs talk the most.

As soon as they came back, we asked for the details.

"You tell," PKC said looking at Tubbs.

"No, no you tell," Tubbs said.

Both of them did this over and again; we got tired and finally announced that if they didn't want to tell then we could always ask the ladies.

"Well… Nothing, they were tourists, that's all," he said and tried to sidetrack us.

"Okay guys… those two girls thought Tubbs was a drug hawker and approached him," PKC spat out the truth.

A couple of 'ohhh' came from all of us.

"The drugged snake! Wah… what a title," I said and hit him hard on the back.

The others too joined me and started teasing Tubbs. He finally lost his cool and went out, but realizing what had just happened, he went back to his room. We somehow pulled him back and consoled him.

After one and half hours, we boarded the bus to go to the pharmacy industry. The colourful pills were of no interest to us, and added to that, we were constantly reminded of safety. All of us looked funny with white aprons on and a mask. We took a quick glance at all the equipment and the conveyor belts loaded with tablets. Of course the formulation and R&D sections were kept at bay and we were not even allowed to venture near.

By the time we returned, it was 10 in the night and as planned, all the guys sneaked out with a bag full of bottles. We went to the beach and some guys were howling loud as if to waken the dead spirits.

We opened the bottles and started drinking; the local Goan liquor hits fast and you get the kick sooner than you think. I was high after two glasses and I started singing out loud and danced to my own music. Soon all the other guys joined me and we moved around hooting like a train and I behaved as if I were the engine. "Chuk chuk chuk chuk coooooooooo…" we screamed and went around in circles.

"Hey staapp… the signal is red…" Roopak said drooling. We saw two policemen arriving with sticks in their hands.

"Chuk chuk chuk chuk coooooooooo… the train has landed on the wrong track; let's move back," I said and turned my 'bogies' in the other direction. Now the police started chasing us. We ran as fast as we could and gave them a hard time.

At last they gave up and warned us in some broken English, "Ayy… I will put you inside I say… Next time I 'finding' you." We sniggered at them and went to our rooms and slept.

One of the guys had mixed this special drink in a bottle of cola. It had got misplaced and accidentally landed among the girls. Unaware of this, we were snoring to glory when someone banged the door; it seemed to go on and on.

"*Arre yaar,* open the door! Bloody killing our sleep!" Tubbs said ducking under the pillow.

"Why don't you do the honours?" someone gurgled, or rather it seemed like one.

"Bloody! Thing man," he said pulling his pajamas and opened the door. And what he saw made his mouth fall like the best gravity experiment ever conducted. Laxmi swamy stood there with a smile; no it was not a smile, it was a grin from ear to ear.

In reflex, Tubbs immediately covered his cheek!

"Okay now, you don't have to stretch the matter. I apologized long back! Okay, I don't mind apologizing again. It was a mistake. I had not 'intendededed' to fall." With great difficulty, he managed to speak these few words.

She still had the smile on her as if it had cost her a million and she wouldn't let it go at any cost. She started swaying and suddenly entered the room and switched on all the lights and threw an empty bottle on the ground.

Everyone in the room woke up with a jolt. The dishevelled look, the half torn clothes or none, made us look like a red-shanked-douc-langur and they started groping at everything they could and managed to cover their assets.

"What did you do now?" I asked looking at Tubbs.

"I swear, I did not; I was just sleeping. I swear to god man, really!" he started.

We looked at the empty bottle and shit! We guessed what might have happened.

"Okay Laxmi why don't you go back to your room ?" Tubbs told her.

She gave a threatening look to Tubbs. He immediately went out to call some girls of our class and resolve the matter. Now, the situation appeared as if a guy barged in the girls' room. We wrenched our faces and were not able to handle this 'delicate' situation.

"She actually looks good without glasses!" someone in the room commented.

"Boss, I know you are drunk. If at all she comes back to her senses, she will create havoc!" SG said as he tried to control our classmates.

"Listen Laxm…" I stopped abruptly unable to believe what was happening in front of us.

"Whoa man, what is happening here?" Tubbs remarked as soon as he came back to the room. "I looked for the girls but they are locked up in a room and refuse to open the door!" he exclaimed, his eyes still very much on Laxmi.

"Shit man, do something before things go awry," I said and tried my best to coax Laxmi to go back. But no, she wouldn't listen to me or any of us. Then she lunged for the laptop thrown on table. "I want to listen to some music!"

"I guess I will have to call the girls myself," I said and again went to their rooms.

"Rashmi, I need your help," I screamed at the top of my lungs. After a lot of "I am sorry," and "Please open the door," she finally opened the door. I asked her to immediately come to our room.

"What is wrong with you?" she shot back.

"I need you to come with me immediately." I dragged her along with me.

"Are you drunk? Oh you are hurting me; leave my hand; why are you misbehaving?" she went on and on.

"Madam, I am not going to hurt you, so just shut up and come," I said and hurried.

We both came to a sudden halt at the scene going on in our room. Laxmi was swinging her arms wildly, to and fro and she had left people around her in a state of coma, nobody had seen her behave so mad before, always composed, and to herself was she and now seeing her so wild and unruly everyone were shocked. Rashmi almost fainted at the sight.

I switched off the music and Rashmi yanked Laxmi hard. She had lost her senses and was in no mood to listen to us.

"I wanttttt too danceee, I am loooovinnng it," she said.

Rashmi paid no heed and took Laxmi away, half coaxing, and pleading her before the professor got a whiff of it.

I looked at my classmates and all I got was a cheeky smile and hungry looks. I closed the door before the dogs could go out on the prowl.

The next day, we went out for shopping. None of the girls accompanied us. We expected that and preferred that to having to face the wrath of the feline community.

When we returned, we had some devilish plans ready for Prajwal Lodi. He was this notorious guy in our class who had troubled most of the girls including Rashmi. This was our only chance to take our revenge as he was away from his other friends.

Prajwal Lodi and two other classmates had occupied the room adjacent to ours. It was late night, about 11. We tiptoed quietly to his room and tried unlocking the door but he had locked it safe and was sleeping.

"Oye Praju, open the door," SG said banging the door so loudly that even a deaf man could have heard this.

We heard some noise and thought maybe Prajwal was coming out. So all set, we made Tubbs stand right in front of the door with *khujili* powder.

The door opened and at that minute the lights went out and all of us barged into the room like wild buffaloes attacking Prajwal.

Tubbs caught hold of him tight and put some powder in his shirt. "Wha..." Prajwal tried to say something but was unable because Tubbs, while doing so, had stepped on Prajwal's leg and the pain was unbearable so he started howling and jumped away. We heard a series of noises one after the other and realized Prajwal had fallen down. Tubbs was trying to bring him up, but he skid over a chappal and fell down with a huge thud!

At that time, the lights came back and to our horrible fates, we realized that it wasn't Prajwal but it was our professor. They had changed rooms. Now we had invited unwanted trouble and all of us were in deep shit!

"Sir...is it you... I mean... we thought Prajwal is staying here..." I said looking as tensed as him.

"You rascals... ah... this huge buffalo lying down nearly killed me..." he said glaring at Tubbs, who had settled comfortably down.

"This is going beyond anybody's control..." He stopped

to scratch his back, and then started a series of "ah... ooohh... what on earth have you put in my shirt?" he asked scratching his back severely.

"Sir... it's a... a... a... medicinal powder...Prajwal was suffering from skin irritation and we thought this will help him." PKC tried to cover the matter.

"Ah... what the hell..." the professor said still scratching his back. He was now looking for something big and handy to scratch the non-reachable areas behind his back.

We thought of helping him and all of us started searching for tools.

"Sir, take this..." Tubbs said handing him a long wooden stick that was lying under the bed.

"Ouch... Ah... give it fast..." he said screaming and partly dancing.

We chuckled, but kept quiet seeing the situation.

Unable to handle it any longer, he ran to the bathroom to have a shower. We thought this was our best chance and escaped to our rooms and stayed put till the next morning.

The next day, we gathered as usual to have our breakfast. All of us were eagerly waiting for the professor. Tubbs pointed towards the entrance; our professor just entered. He didn't look at anyone. With a stern face he directly went to the buffet and started putting food on his plate.

We still had our eyes on him. Word had spread to the entire class and all of us watched each move of his as if he was some alien.

After loading his plate sufficiently, he went to the corner

and started nibbling. He was way too normal after what happened yesterday. For a full ten minutes we watched his moves with interest, but nothing unusual happened, so disappointed, we all started gobbling our food. Then the action started. He balanced his plate on one hand and desperately tried to reach his spine; in that attempt, some food spilled on the ground. To avoid this, he stood against the wall and started rubbing his back against it. All of us looked at him. The professor looked at us and we immediately kept quiet.

He then took his plate and went to his room to have breakfast. That was probably the heights of troubling a professor. We then decided not to play such pranks that could end up on a serious note. So, Roopak and I took some ointment and handed it to Prajwal and told him to go and give it to the professor.

Later that day, we got to know that he was feeling much better. We were glad that it didn't lead to anything serious and heaved a sigh of relief. Because of his problem, we had cancelled our outing and stayed in our rooms playing and watching movies.

In the evening, we went to the professor's room and apologized for whatever happened. To our relief, he gladly welcomed us and started chatting. By the end of two hours, we got very close.

In the evening, there was a surprise for all of us. The professor had arranged for a camp fire at night. All of us eagerly waited for the night to arrive.

It was a breezy night and was perfectly set for a campfire night. We guys had gone there a bit early. The management had arranged for a DJ and he was scoring nice music.

All of us started grooving to his numbers and the night was turning out to be better. The girls arrived late, as was their habit. They were looking as pretty as ever. I looked out for Rashmi, but when I couldn't find her, I joined my friends and started dancing round the fire.

Then someone just nudged me. I turned around to see none other than Rashmi! Oh I was so happy that for a few seconds, I just kept staring at her to see whether she had really come or I was dreaming.

She gave me a small punch and pulled me out of that state. "Mind if I join you…" she asked.

"Oh please, by all means," I said smiling back at her.

All my friends started calling my name. "*Kya baat hain Zahir…! Man what moves…*"

Both of us were looking at each other and dancing, well not exactly, but swinging ourselves to the music. I wanted to talk to her so desperately but the crowd and the music distracted my desires. "I want to talk to you," I whispered into her ears. Before she could even react, I just dragged her out of the crowd and went aside.

"Let's go for a walk," I said. She simply nodded and walked with me towards the beach.

She was wearing a white *salwar* with blue flowers on it. She was continually adjusting her *dupatta* and thanks to the breeze, every time she set it right, the breeze spoilt it. She wore a small *jumkha* and had left her tresses at the mercy of the wind. As I walked, I could smell the perfume and that made me go weak every second.

"So you wanted to talk," she said not looking at me.

"I…. uh… nothing," I said, and then said, "No …I want

to talk… Why the hell didn't you talk to me all these days? It's been more than three months since we spoke. What went wrong?" I said sounding very serious now. She was still looking down. "I am sorry; I know what I did was wrong, but I had to do it. There was no other way."

"What do you mean?"

"I tried to stay away from you. I forced myself not to talk or be in touch with you any longer."

"And what's this stupidity for?"

"Well, you confronted the entire college for my sake, I mean; I was honestly bowled over by that act of yours. I knew you were getting very close to me and I wanted to avoid this…"

"Well… could you?"

"No… I couldn't do that any longer…" she said. At that moment, a strand of hair flew on her forehead and her bangles clinked as she tried to push it back. The night was perfect, the sea roared as we walked along the shore. The moonlight sprawled across the never-ending shore. The wind whispered love, the sea roared love. We let our feet feel the sand; we sunk and rose with every step, the sand rolled on our feet unravelling but promising to be back. We started playing against each other's feet and after a while, we just walked in silence and at times, when my hand touched hers, she became uncomfortable, but I was eagerly waiting for more such occurrences.

"You are beautiful," I said breaking the silence.

"Thanks." She blushed.

"You have gorgeous hair",I said looking at her.

She just looked down and again said, "Thanks." This time I could see her blush more and the sides of her cheek resembled a budding rose.

"Can we go now?" she said feeling very shy.

"No wait… let's go near the beach," I said. We went near and I could see her thinking. She had this half smile on her face as she walked with me.

"Doesn't the sea resemble our life? One never knows what lies beneath. The hidden treasures or the hidden feelings," I said looking at her deeply.

"I agree," she said and smiled back at me.

This was the most beautiful moment of my life. I don't remember when I was this happy before. I just wanted to hug her like this throughout my life and never let her go. We sat on the beach,letting ourselves at the whims of the waves. We sat there for a long time gazing at the stars . Neither of us spoke a word, strange though it may seem, the world stood still. I loved every second of it. So many unspoken words yet every word was understood, the feelings were so clear yet they weren't spoken. The charm of the moment was not in being told , but was in feeling it with every passage of time. We both were in a trance and embraced the moment, but then we could hear somebody shout and abruptly we were pulled to this world again.

I looked at her and could see that she was relaxed and calm.as if to say some burden had been removed from her shoulders and this pleased me She smiled at me and said "Zahir lets go"

I went to the room directly and went to sleep.

The morning appeared sooner than expected. All of

us felt bad that our happy days had come to an end. With a heavy heart, we packed our bags and loaded the luggage in our bus.

Rashmi seemed normal now and smiled at me. I too smiled back but then wondered if that smile was for me. I turned back to see if someone behind me was the recipient of the smile, but no, it was meant for me. She laughed when she saw my confused act.

People looking out for mysteries should try understanding women. If you are successful, buddy, you have hit the nail on the head.

Anyways, this time I reacted normally and didn't reach the seventh heaven when she smiled because the travel time from there back to the ground was hardly a few seconds when dealing with occupants of Venus.

We took our seats and there was not much *josh* left. Some people sang and the others stuck to their windows. I put on the iPod and slept. We finally bade farewell to the land of babes and beaches.

CHAPTER 10
SECOND INNINGS

Our semesters started again and all was back to normal - the boring lectures and the internals. But we were waiting for the cultural day in our college.

Now, before you readers wonder whether we study or only party the entire time, let me tell you, I am just giving you a glimpse of the green pastures of our college life. Studies and all *kya yaar*; you wouldn't want me to mention about them, would you?

"This is the height of culture," I said astonished.

"What do you mean?" Roopak followed my gaze.

A group of people were carrying guns and daggers and their attire depicted Indian movie dacoits. They wore a mask covering their mouth and a big black turban around their head with a big leather belt around the belly.

Some lecturers gave them a hard stare.

"Look at them! This is supposed to be a culture day and these boys have dressed like goons," one professor commented on the gang.

But the entire gang remained unfazed by these comments. The entire college welcomed them with whistles and hoots.

"Hey guys, what are you planning to do for tomorrow?" Tubbs came running at us. He was breathing heavily.

"Are you getting married or what? And by the way, who in this world is marrying you, man?" Roopak asked giving a hi-five to me.

"Tomorrow is Rose Day," he said looking at us, still unable to recover from breathlessness.

"This is your last chance, Zahir," Roopak said looking at me.

"What about my Rosy darling?" Tubbs interrupted.

"Who? That oversized Rosy?" Roopak said and started laughing at the top of his voice. Tubbs' face showed a tinge of dejection.

"Okay, tell me Zahir, are you going to propose or should I propose if you don't?" Roopak asked again focusing his attention on me.

"No, I can't do it. I know the answer," I said in a symbolic manner raising my hands and eyebrows.

Of course, I had not told my friends what happened in Goa. I wasn't sure if she had forgotten that, but me, I was living every second in those blissful moments.

"Wait," I said searching for Rashmi in the huge crowd that had gathered near the main function hall. But I couldn't find her.

"Aren't you attending the speech?" Ram, our classmate, called us.

"Na, we don't listen to others' speech; we make our own," Roopak said.

Ram just gave a confused look and walked away.

"So today is wasted *haan*?" Tubbs asked.

"Yeah, who the hell wants to listen to speech and all?"

I said referring to the introductory annual function speech given by our principal.

"Okay let's go back; I am feeling hungry and this is the last bus," Tubbs said catching his stomach.

"I don't think there is any day this person has been without food," Roopak said and put a hand on my shoulder.

"I don't know how he keeps up with his fast during Ramzan; unbelievable," I said putting one hand on Tubbs and other on Roopak's shoulder.

"Okay, we will meet tomorrow." I bade goodbye to Tubbs and Roopak and got down at my stop.

The next day was our 'College Annual Day'. All girls were wearing saris and guys had to be dressed in a suit with a tie. Since I owned no suit, I thought I can take help of my senior

I banged the door of one of my seniors

"Who's that? What the hell do you need?" my senior in the hostel yelled.

"Sir, Zahir here."

"Oh champ, come in, what's up?" he opened the door and ushered me in.

"Sir, I wanted a favour from you," I asked meekly.

"What's it champ, tell me," he asked me gesturing me to sit.

"Sir, I need your suit and tie for the annual day."

"That's it? I thought we had to bash somebody. So it's about girls and all that *haan*…" he teased me.

"No, sir I have to follow the protocol. All my friends will be dressed for this occasion."

"What happened to your *chamiya*? Are you still in love

with her?" he asked.

"Actually sir…"

"Come on boss, I know your story; just go ahead and propose to her."

"I am afraid of rejection," I said speaking my heart out.

"She can't say 'no' to you," he assured me.

"But I am planning not to propose to her."

"Just think about it; you might never get another chance in life again."

I collected the suit and the tie from my senior and went to college.

It was a three-piece black suit, not Armani, but a good one. It had a black waist coat with a midnight grey tie, that complemented each other perfectly. I wore nice shoes and put on my cologne which I had saved for occasions. I checked myself in the mirror and went to college.

The annual day function started at 6 in the evening with dance performances, songs and skits. I had decided to give them a miss and joined the dance party that was held later in the evening.

"Hi handsome," Roopak said from behind and looked at me from tip to toe. "Looking good…"

"But what happened to your eyes? They seem dull," Roopak asked.

"I am fine, just that I was unable to sleep because of mosquitoes."

"Is it mosquitoes or …" Roopak smiled at me.

"Come on *yaar*, I have decided not to propose."

"Okay boss your wish; I have tried my best to convince you," Roopak said giving up.

We both entered the dance hall.

"Come, let's go to the dance floor. Let's have some fun," Roopak said and pulled me to the floor although I was reluctant.

Tubbs, SG and PKC were already on the floor dancing to the music.

"Look who's that?" Roopak said.

"Oh man, what a scene! I can't believe my eyes." I started rubbing my eyes.

"Is it a dream?" Roopak pinched me.

"Is it Shastry? Are you sure?" I was gaping at him.

"Come on Zahir, this is a shame. When Shastry can dance, why can't you?" Roopak forced.

"You go ahead." I pushed Roopak and went to the song dedication area.

The host announced, "This song is dedicated to Rashmi from Zahir."

"*Pehla nasha, pehla khumar…*"

"What the hell? Who has dedicated this song?" I said listening to it.

Tubbs waved his hand from the juke box corner.

"Come on, you cannot do this." I threw my hands up in the air.

Suddenly my eye caught something shimmering at the entrance. I saw a girl wearing a nice glittering sari, her long black silky hair swayed flirtatiously. She wore beautiful earrings with green stone embedded in the centre of the ring. And hugging her was a black sari with a golden *zari* and towering heels supported her tender feet. And it perfectly complemented her height. She tried to put her hair behind her ears with her beautiful hands. While doing so, I could see her neatly manicured fingernails painted with the stroke of pinkish nail polish with a tinge of brown colour on it. It was shining beautifully. She had a black bag which suited her sari.

The lights emphasized her silhouette showing a perfect figure.

"Wow beautiful", I said when I saw her, the only word that hovered around me was 'beautiful'!

I called Roopak. "Pull out your smelly socks; I need to know if I am sober!"

"What?" muttered Roopak. "Have you gone crazy?"

"*Nahi yaar*, is that Rashmi?" I asked him pointing at her.

"Wow, soooo…wow, yes it is Rashmi." Roopak had his mouth open.

"I have changed my mind," I said unable to take my eyes off her.

"About what?" Roopak asked inquisitively.

"I am going to propose to her, but…"

"But what?" Roopak asked looking at her.

"Look, that *chindi chor* is lurking around her since such a long time," I said looking at Prajwal Pogaria; he too had shown some interest in my girl.

"Don't worry; why the hell has Tubbs been born in this world for?" Roopak assured me patting my back.

Roopak went and told Tubbs about this.

"Pogaaaaaaaaaria, Princi is calling you," Tubbs said pointing towards the principal's room.

"Why is he calling me now? You don't understand, I am with Rashmi," Prajwal said irritated.

"He was talking about some placements abroad," Tubbs bluffed.

"Oh great, that's cool. I will come in five minutes, Rashmi," he said and ran towards the principal's office.

"Wait, wait…" Tubbs also followed him.

"He asked you to get your certificates, mark sheets and all academic stuff, so you'd better go to your room and get all these."

"Oh… but… okay no problem. I'll go right away," he said and galloped away like a horse.

"Hi Rashmi, how are you?" I was in total awe.

She hit me with her bag. "Where were you? I was searching for you since such a long time."

"I was here; I wanted to talk to you but…" I stopped.

"But what?"

"That Pooooogaria was with you," I said.

She laughed and said, "He was gassing around with his illogical talk; he might come back anytime."

"Don't worry, he will never trouble you today again," I told her.

"Rashmi… Do you know how pretty you are? I am totally lost in you today. You are looking so beautiful and so hot," I said looking deep in her eyes.

"Thanks," she said and blushed.

"And this is for you," I said and pulled out a red rose and gave it to her. I was shy.

"Well… thanks again," she said smelling the rose.

"Were you expecting this from me?" I asked.

"Of course," she said.

"I wanted to tell…" Before I could tell her something,

she pulled me in the crowd.

"Come on, let's dance," she was shouting and singing along with the juke box.

"Not bad, you dance well," I bent and screamed in her ears.

"Yeah, I am a professional dancer," she shouted back.

"I am a bathroom dancer," I said laughing.

"So what? Everyone here is a bathroom dancer; just keep dancing, and don't worry."

"Yeah true," I said but was feeling uneasy because I could not tell her what I wanted to. So I broke off from the dance floor.

Making up my mind, I went back to her.

"Can you please come outside for a moment?" I shouted in her ears.

"Why?"

"Please, I need to talk to you."

"You can tell me, I am listening," she said still dancing.

"No, I can't talk to you here; please come outside," I said and left.

She followed me.

"I wanted to tell you that…" Before I could complete my sentence, someone said, "Hi Rashmi, you are looking good." It was one of her friends in her group.

"Thanks, you too," Rashmi screamed back.

'Please God, don't allow them to come here,' I was praying.

"Let's go and hip hop." Her friend forced her and again they dragged her to the dance floor.

I couldn't bear this happening the second time and I went to the cafeteria.

"One Coke please," I requested the cafeteria guy.

"Yes sir, one moment," he said.

I started thinking about how to approach her and tell her. She was dancing and looking at me all the time. I completed the cold drink and went to the DJ who was banging his head in the air.

"Mickey, please take down this dedication to Rashmi."

"Which song man?"

I thought for a while and said, "Forget about it." I could not gather the strength to dedicate the song. I went back to the cafeteria again.

"One more Coke please," I ordered and drank it within no time.

My heart was beating even faster. I again went to the song dedication section.

"Mickey, can you give me the mike? I want to make an announcement."

"Yes sure; only after the next dedication. Please wait for a minute," he said and announced the next dedication.

"Take the mike." Mickey extended his hand.

"Hello everyone… check check… I am Zahir here and I need to make an important announcement." I trembled as I said these words. Now the entire crowd became attentive.

"This is for you, Rashmi."

I asked them to switch off the lights and focus on her. Now the lights were only on her and I could see that she was quite shocked.

"I am not an actor, a poet or a writer. I cannot make phrases, sentences or actions. But I am a joker who will make you laugh when you are sad, I am the pillar that will hold you strong when you need, I am the anchor that will keep you calm amidst trouble. And I will promise you that not this second, not this minute, but I will love you till eternity. I love you Rashmi.

If love is a star, I present you the sky
If love is dew, I present you the rain
If love is a flower, I present you a bouquet
But if love is you,
All I can say is please be mine!
One wish, one desire, one hope
One thought, one reason, one prayer
That you will be mine, not for today or now
But forever and ever!"

The minute I said this, the entire crowd cheered and some even whistled. I just looked at Rashmi to see her reaction. My heart was in my mouth. Never was I so tensed in my life. My life was in that answer; it could make or break me.

Uff! How she looked. With her head bent down and that shy smile, she looked at me. I could see her eyes filled with tears. She just nodded her head and said "Yes."

The whole crowd roared in joy. I just stood there not knowing how to react. It was like a piece of heaven presented to me. I was completely at a loss to say anything. For the first time in my life I thanked God, I thanked my stars. My happiness knew no boundaries that day. I felt like running towards her and hugging her tight.

My friends lifted me up and danced around. Finally I was allowed to go and stand beside her. The whole crowd had gone berserk.

"So…" I said smiling at Rashmi.

"So…?" she asked me with a huge smile on her face.

"I mean… you liked it?" I asked.

"Yeah… it was very romantic," she said trying to look away from my eyes.

Barely had the conversation started when everyone pushed us for a dance. A soft romantic number was dedicated to both of us. The song 'A groovy kind of love' by Phil Collins floated in the air and held us as if it were a magnet.

I held her tight and both of us started grooving to this number slowly and all the couples in our college too joined us. It was the second best night in my life.

After the dance, I dropped her to her place. Both of us experienced a strange bond that made it difficult for us to let go of each other. With love filled in my heart, I went to my hostel and slept peacefully.

The next few days were so blissful. We would meet and stay together the entire day. I was sure that both of us were made for each other. It was like all the romantic songs in Bollywood were meant for us.

This period was short-lived because the final examinations were just round the corner and we had to struggle to get a decent score.

It was so difficult to concentrate on studying.

Heat transfer (one of our main subjects in chemical engineering) would become thought transfer, and both of us would call and talk for hours, since study holidays were declared prior to the exam.

She would force me to study at least for the sake of impressing her dad. She was very close to her dad and a typical 'daddy's girl'. I would sometimes wonder what her decision would be if her dad asked, "Zahir or me?"

'Anyway, right now the moment is to enjoy and not worry about the future; somehow I will manage to convince the other man in my girl's life,' I would pacify myself.

It was ten days before the exam when Rashmi called me up to say, "Zahir, we need to talk…" Her voice sounded very different. I thought she was worried about her exams.

"*Yaar*, please don't worry; you will do well in your exams, I am sure. If I am disturbing you then I will cut down the calls," I tried assuring her.

"No… it's not about the exam! It's about us…" she said, her tone unusually low.

"Sweetu, what is bothering you? What happened?" I asked her. Now I too was a bit tensed.

"Actually last night *baba* overheard me talking over phone and this morning he asked me. I couldn't lie to him… so… I told him about us."

"And…" I gulped hard.

"And… he said he will not allow me to write exams if he hears me talking to you again…"

"Did he comment on my being a Muslim?"

"Well…"

"Okay, no need to explain; don't worry, everything will be fine. You just concentrate on your studies now. Let's see what the future has planned for us." I tried my best to comfort her.

"No, Zahir, it is not that simple. He asked me to…" she started crying over phone.

My heart wrenched to hear her cry. *"Jaan*... listen... please stop crying. I will do something about it, don't worry. Please don't cry. I cannot see you hurt."

"Zahir... I think we should separate..."

I actually took sometime to realize she was saying this to me. Initially I felt she was saying all this emotionally, but she was determined about ending this relationship. No matter what I said, it fell on deaf ears. So helplessly, I agreed to part ways.

That day I went to the bar. I was dejected and wanted to come out of it. I drank till I could no longer think; probably I was the last customer in the bar. The next day I got to know that Roopak had got me to my hostel. I was so drunk that I had lost control on my mind and the bartender had found Roopak's number in my cell and contacted him.

I was absolutely not in a mood to study.

"Have you completed your studies?" Roopak asked me.

"I don't even know what to study."

"If you don't clear, then your whole stats will go for a toss." Roopak was worried looking at me. I had told him about Rashmi's call yesterday.

"Who cares? I don't have any reason to study."

"Aren't you bothered about your parents at least? Come on man, don't be such a loser in life," Roopak said trying to elevate my mood.

"I just don't know; please do not disturb me; go away," I pleaded to him.

Then I realized with how much difficulty my dad and mom had saved money to sponsor my education. They had to curb their desires to fulfil mine. It was true that I never spent their money with disdain. I would always think twice before shelling out any bucks. Although I didn't do well in my first two semesters, I improved tremendously in my other semesters. I had brilliantly picked up the subjects of chemical engineering and had always showed up in the top three slots in the class.

I had to do more than just being appreciative for their undying support throughout my education. It would be really stupid of me if I wasted the year because of a girl.

I realized there was no point in mourning and decided to leave the old for good. So I resolved to put my anger and frustration behind me and concentrate on my studies. Having decided this, I went to Roopak's house.

"Sorry," I said looking at him.

"Manners and all *haan;* bloody get your ass in," he said and hugged me.

"How are you guys planning your studies?" I asked.

"We are going to SG's house as usual," Roopak said asking me to get the books from the hostel.

We studied for the next nine days doing night outs and slogged to complete the syllabus. We referred to the old question papers and solved them thoroughly; this had become my secret tool of scoring in the exams.

All our exams went very well. After our last exam got over, we started planning how to celebrate. Suddenly, Rashmi came and stood in front of me and said, "I want to talk to you."

"What is it about?" I asked trying to be as calm as possible.

"Can you give me some precious time of yours?"

"Okay!" I said and we walked towards the college canteen.

Rashmi started, "Please talk to me."

"How did your exams go?" I asked looking at my bike key.

"Okay; I will manage to clear the papers," she said touching my hand on the table.

"I cannot think of any other person in my life. The last few days were hell. I couldn't bear the separation. I love you Zahir. I want to be yours and only yours."

"What?" I asked in total dismay and looked at her staring straight into her eyes.

"I desperately want to be with you; let's elope," she said.

"Have you gone crazy?" I yelled at her.

"Why? What's wrong? I am choosing my life. I love my parents, no doubt about that. But I cannot stay without you. They are looking for a groom and by hook or crook they will force me to marry," she said.

"Listen Rashmi, I will convince your parents somehow. Please let's not take this route."

"No I am not going to listen to anyone. I have decided and I am going to stick to it. If I don't marry you then I will commit suicide!" she threatened.

"Idiot! Have you gone out of your senses? Don't you dare talk recklessly about life! Face the world, be bold," I said sternly.

"Then you tell me what I should do. I am feeling so helpless."

"Okay, give me some time to think about it, and then

we will decide. Till then, I want you to act sensible and don't make a mess out of your life; clear?"

I immediately rushed to my friends after sending Rashmi home. All of them were eagerly waiting for my return; they asked if everything was fine. I told them what had transpired between Rashmi and me and wanted their help in making my decision.

"Oh god, what to do now?" Tubbs said scratching his chin.

"Whatever decision you take, we are with you, Zahir," SG said and everyone agreed.

"Okay guys, thanks a lot. I want your support," I said taking a deep breath.

"When will you be meeting her?" Roopak asked.

"Fifty days from today. I don't know what is right or wrong but it's a 'do or die' situation for me. I still need to get a job, if we elope; I need to make some basic arrangements. And we have to get married immediately."

"Isn't this a bit too much? I mean, is there no way of convincing her parents?" SG said thoughtfully.

"Boss, in India people are valued by their religion, not by their values. And thanks to my background, I will get butchered if I venture anywhere near her house. They supposedly belong to the elite category. I don't understand all this. The heart and virtue are nowhere in the picture; caste and creed and language are important. When some calamity occurs, will it ask what religion you are and then take a call on whether it should affect you? It's high time people give this a thought," I said hoping that in the near future, one doesn't have to think so much before loving or marrying.

"Anyways, let's go back. I want to think and then come to a conclusion about this entire thing," I said and all of us parted and decided to meet the next day.

I went back to the hostel. I thought about it all day. I was restless. Was it the right thing to do? I thought about my parents, the sacrifices they made all their life for me. My love was overpowering everything. My heart ruled over my mind at that time. I was known to have very good emotional control, but now I was undecided.

The next day, I went to Roopak and said, "You remember Parvez *bhai?* We had helped him during the youth festival to get his candidate win."

"So what?" Roopak got up.

"We will go and meet him."

"You are going to make a politically religious issue out of this matter; you know that Rashmi's father is a political stalwart in this area."

"No *yaar*, we will not go into all these things." I got up.

"We will ask him to arrange for a decent shelter and a job if possible in Mumbai. We will ask him to make sure that nobody finds out about our whereabouts. Meanwhile, I will get my degree certificate and find a job.

"*Salam bhai,*" I said to Parvez *bhai* on entering his house. He was a well-known *gunda* in Belgaum.

Parvez Basha was the son of a butcher. His father had ten mouths to feed other than himself and his spouse. So his upbringing was nothing much to mention other than the survival battle that he had to undergo. Not so good at studies, he decided to make a career of his own.

That led him to politics. He was huge, say about 6 feet tall, well built and had the frame of a man weighing around 200 pounds. He was in his late forties and wore a long white *Kurta* with a gold bracelet dangling in his wrist. Ten rings sat on his fingers, all pure gold mind you! Constantly chewing beetle leaves had turned his mouth red. Some people said that he carried a gun, but in the public's eye, he was a poor man's hope. Contrary to his image, he was very generous with poor people and helped them magnanimously. He had come to our college for the local secretary elections and we had helped his candidate to win.

"*Salam*, oh you are that student who helped me in the youth festival." He asked us to come in.

"*Bhai*, I need some help."

"Yes tell me," he said chewing *paan* like a cow chewing the never-ending cud.

"*Bhai*…" I stopped since I was not used to the formalities one has to follow when talking to 'big' people.

He seemed to notice this and said, "I get angry when people consider themselves low. I like it when they are more open."

When I didn't respond, he said, "Tell me, someone bothering you?"

"No *bhai*, actually it's a girl."

"So the matter is here," he said poking my chest.

"Hmmm difficult… in all my years of experience, only once have I failed and that is this subject. Very difficult it is," he said pacing from one end of the room to the other.

He had three body guards; one look at them is sufficient

to make you dizzy. They stood rock solid watching our every move. One wrong step and I am sure they would knock us out by their piercing looks.

"I know *bhai* and that's why we have decided to elope to Mumbai," I said wondering whether it was too much to ask. "And for that I need your help."

"What help and who is the girl?"

"I need an accommodation in Mumbai and a job too and by the way, the girl is Joshi's daughter."

"Which Joshi?" he said suddenly halting mid way.

"*Bhai*, Hitler Joshi's."

Everybody immediately stood up. Parvez *Bhai* caught hold of me by the collar and dragged me to throw me out of his house.

"Just get lost, you fool. Do you know what you are talking about? You are talking about bloodbath."

"I know, I know that you are a man of principles."

"No boy, you don't realize; don't underestimate him. He has his wings spread everywhere. My deadliest enemy, but a worthy opponent."

"I have neither job nor that kind of huge amount to take care of her right now. I will be grateful if you could help me find a job within this short span. My interview results are due after three months and I cannot wait for that long," I beseeched him.

He thought for sometime but he was still unwilling to lend me any support. Since all my requests failed, I decided to find my own way.

"No problem *bhai*, thanks for your time. Small people like us are not so privileged to meet great people like you. We are happy that you gave us some time," I said and we stood up to leave.

"No wait…" he said and took out his flashy mobile phone.

"Yeah, it's me. Matter is urgent. Ask Sultan to talk to me immediately," he said. We all stood quietly.

Suddenly the phone rang. "Hello, listen. One kid here needs a job, he is a…"

"What's your branch, I forgot," he asked me.

"Chemical *bhai*."

"… yeah a chemical engineer. No, not chemicals, CHEMICAL ENGINEER. Correct. So find a job in Mumbai and even a decent place to stay. Call me back immediately." He disconnected the call and said, "Don't worry kid, I am not that bad, but one needs to gauge a character before helping. People tend to be rude when their help is unanswered, but you were humble and that is what is important, my boy. Now be at ease; I will call you tomorrow."

"Thanks *bhai*, thanks a ton. I am a self-made man but because of the urgency I had to seek your help. I will remain in debt throughout my life for this help. I know he is your bitter enemy. I am sorry to put you into trouble. The relation may get harder between you two and I am responsible for this…"

"Dear boy, leave the rest to me. I know how to handle the situation. Just stay with the girl and don't break her trust," he said smiling.

After receiving his assurance, I left peacefully. How often we judge people going by hearsay. I was sceptical to approach him thinking my reputation also would be at stake, but after knowing what sort of a man he was, I realized that he was a true gentleman at heart and only situations had made him what he was now.

The same evening he called me and said, "Make sure that this does not go out of this building. I will give you the address and other details about Mumbai."

"Thank you *bhai*, I will never forget your favour," I said. The call ended with a word of advice.

I shifted all my belongings from my hostel to my house. My parents were elated to see me and received me warmly. I had a royal treatment for a few days. I missed talking to Rashmi but nothing could be done since she had warned me strictly not to call.

Ten more days were left for the D-day. SG called me and my other friends and asked us to meet at our usual hangout near college. The two-hour drive hardly bothered me, as I was excited to meet my buddies.

I reached early and was waiting for them; all my college day memories flooded my mind. It was a small tea stall just beside the college with an old wooden plank laid outside.

I was looking over a building nearby at the tea stall where we made a dash one day to answer nature's call. I smiled to myself at that thought.

"Hey bro, how are you?" SG and PKC called from behind. I stood up and gave them a warm hug. It was *so good to be with friends.*

"Hey I am fine; how are you guys doing?" I gushed happily.

"Yeah great, I am still enjoying my honeymoon period," PKC said.

"Bloody, I have to go to my fields in a village," SG said

looking up with a sigh.

"But I am enjoying good food and rest," Tubbs joined in with a bigger looking tummy.

"Tubbs, bloody, what have you done to yourself man? No wonder Bush commented about India's food consumption," Roopak said fondling Tubbs' belly.

"Owners pride neighbours envy! Huh," Tubbs defended himself. All of us laughed at this.

"Did Roopak tell you about my plans?" I asked excitedly.

"Yes, we wanted to talk to you regarding this." SG put his hand on my back. "That is why we thought of this get together."

"Zahir, how well do you know Rashmi?" SG asked as a matter of fact.

"What sort of a question is this? Don't you guys know her?" I said, perplexed at the question being thrown at me.

"Answer us, it's serious," SG said looking at me.

"What's the matter?" I asked him.

"SG, why are you beating around the bush? Just tell him straight. Zahir, leave her, she is not good for you," PKC interrupted.

"What is wrong with you guys?" I said standing up.

"Zahir, please listen to us and don't be an emotional fool. We know the truth and we are trying to bring it out," PKC said not losing his composure.

"Do you realize what you are saying? I have been in love with her since the day I saw her and it's been more than four years. It's no puppy love. I am damn serious about her and we are planning to elope in a week's time," I said defiantly.

"We came to know that she has an affair with someone else and…"

"And what?" I was very furious. "You guys amaze me. I thought you guys supported our relation all through the college days and now what I get to hear is this crap! Look guys, I know her better than any of you okay? I know she is not having an affair with anyone; maybe she was talking to some guy and that aroused a doubt in your minds. But please let's not discuss this. I will not appreciate any talk about her." My anger grew more with every word I spoke.

"Cool down," PKC tried to console me.

"How much do you guys know her, you bastards," I started shouting.

"Zahir, you are crossing the limits. We didn't cook this story out of blue. PKC and I saw her at a coffee shop with some guy and forget it, I cannot explain any more," SG said harshly.

"What did you see?" I demanded thumping my fist on the table.

"I cannot say this; I am sure you will not believe us and I don't want our relationship to go sour. Why don't you ask your girl friend?" I could sense some sarcasm involved and this enraged me to an extent of grabbing PKC by the collar and shoving him hard.

"Please! Not a word against Rashmi," I warned him.

Roopak who had been silent all this while pulled me aside and said, "Zahir, I knew this long back but was hesitant to tell you. I vouch for PKC and I too know the truth about Rashmi. I guess it's better you talk to her once. We are not your enemies and want the best to happen, but the truth is hard; you got to accept it or if you still have doubts, please talk to her about this."

"Just fuck off, otherwise..." I left the place without looking at them and I knew that it was the end of my relationship with everybody.

"Zahir wait, please, it's for your good," Roopak shouted.

"Come on don't leave us and go," SG shouted.

I kept on walking and never turned back...

I called Rashmi immediately, but my calls went unanswered so I left a message asking her to contact me. I waited for three days and didn't get a single call. I ignored my friends' calls and didn't bother to talk with Roopak either. One week passed without any reply from her. Now with only three days left to elope, I wondered if my friends had told me the truth. But I was still confident about my love and assured myself that all this was a bad dream and it would pass.

Finally the day arrived; we had decided to meet at 10 in the morning. That meant I had to leave my house at 7.30. I was up by 4 and reworked my plans, and also spoke to Parvez *bhai* about the arrangements. Everything was set; I went downstairs and peeped into my parents' room. My dad was still asleep and mom was busy preparing tea.

"*Maa*, I need to go out for some work. I will get back in a few days," I said.

"What? Now? Why didn't you tell us before? Which place? How far it is? When are you coming?" my mother asked coming out of the kitchen.

"Please hold on; if you ask so many questions at one go, how will I answer? I am going to Pondicherry for training and it may take one year to complete it. I had applied to that institution long back and I got the reply yesterday and they have asked me to join from the fourth, that is three days from today!" I said avoiding any sort of eye contact.

"Oh nice! Why did you tell us now? You should have given this information after reaching there. After all, what are we? Useless old people, right?" she said annoyingly.

"*Maa*...I am sorry I didn't expect this call. It was unexpected and I will be coming every weekend for sure," I coaxed her.

"And thanks for informing us in advance," she added sarcastically.

"Now please don't start off your emotional drama. Even I got to know yesterday; okay I will pack now; I have to leave in sometime," I said and sprinted to my room.

I came downstairs with my baggage and called my mother. She came along with my dad and after a lot of 'call-us eat-properly' etc., I left the house. I felt guilty for not being honest with my parents. But I had already made up my mind and now backing out would lead us nowhere. I decided to make it up later with my parents.

I reached the decided spot and waited for her. I tried calling her, but she didn't respond. I waited for more than two hours; still she didn't turn up. The sun was high and harsh with every passing second. After four hours, I became impatient and dashed to her house.

I was exhausted and very hungry; it was almost two in the afternoon. Nothing came to my mind except her. I was angry with her for not making a call or responding. But I was wondering whether our plans were nipped and whether her parents had come to know about this .With all this confusion and anxiety, I walked towards her house. I almost reached her house, and what I saw was a bolt out of the blue. She was standing on the terrace and chatting gaily with some guy. I could see it was more than a friendly chat. I didn't believe my eyes and closer. When she saw me, the colour faded from her face. She immediately ran downstairs and came out of the house and pulled me aside.

"What are you doing here? I asked you not to come or contact me," she said hurriedly.

"Am I talking to Rashmi? What the hell do you mean by this? Don't you remember our plan?" I asked her.

"I know, I know, but I need some more time. I am still not ready for this," she said without any hint of guilt.

At this point, my temper reached sky high. "Are you kidding me? Bloody, it was you who hatched this plan and now you are behaving as if I have created this. And you didn't even have the courtesy to inform me about this?"

"I couldn't; my cell was snatched from me and my mother was constantly near the land line, so I never got a chance to call you," she said looking cautiously everywhere.

"So now we are not eloping?" I knitted my brows at this point.

"Please go now; I don't want to be spotted by my parents

or neighbours. I will try calling you by tomorrow," she said hardly showing any interest about me what-so-ever.

"So, who is that guy?" I said pointing towards the roof top of her house.

"That…is.."she struggled for words when I asked her.

"Zahir, don't talk to me or call me for a few days. I will explain everything to you later."

"I insist madam Rashmi! Who is that guy and are you really serious about us? I have already made arrangements in Mumbai, even secured a good job!"

"Zahir, I think we have to call off our relationship. I am not sure I can live a decent life hurting my parents."

"Are you playing with my life? Just when I was regaining from the break up, you came from nowhere and said all those big words about love and eloping. I think I was a fool to believe you, thanks for making my life more miserable, and whoever that guy is, please don't spoil his life!" I don't remember all that I spoke; it was worse than a nightmare.

'God! Why is all this happening to me? Because of this, I lost my friends, I didn't even trust them,' I thought as I walked back towards my house. It was like life had played a cruel joke at me. I locked myself in the house for the next one month. If I heard any word on love or friendship, I would become fidgety.

My parents noticed my behaviour and tried talking to me about this, but in vain. I neither spoke nor reacted. It was like a state of coma.

I decided to rewrite my fate. I was not destined to wither away like maple leaves. I made up my mind to let go of the past. In order to do so, I had to move out of this place. As they say, familiarity breeds contempt. My situation didn't look any better.

I still had one option left, that is, go to Mumbai and make a life for myself. After talking to Parvez *bhai* and updating him about my not-so-good life, he assured me that the job was still intact and I could join if I intended. I grabbed this opportunity and set off to Mumbai.

CHAPTER 11
CAT OUT OF THE BAG

"That is the last I heard from Zahir. We looked for him everywhere, and even his parents shifted their house. We scanned all the social networking sites – Orkut, Facebook, Twitter – in vain," Roopak said gravely.

We were so engrossed in Zahir's narration that we never realized how time flew. I had never expected Zahir's life to be so heartrending. I now realized why he had retreated in a shell. His life had many upheavals.

Zahir's story had an unmistaken resemblance to that of my distant cousin. I recollected that there was a small tiff in the family concerning a Muslim guy. Since I was very young, the elders had kept me at bay regarding this matter.

Holy love! Zahir was none other than my cousin Rashmi's so-called boy friend! The earth beneath my feet shook at this thought.

Then Roopak got a call. He had to rush immediately to see his ailing mother.

"Zahir, I got to go. Give me your number. I have to tell you something important." Roopak took Zahir's number and left.

My eyes filled with tears when I remembered my cousin. 'Oh god, did they reject this guy who is worth a million!' My heart filled with hatred towards my cousin's parents. They had no idea what they had lost in life! For a second, I blamed this world which divided people in innumerable ways!

I was left with no words. I refrained from crying. My emotions were taking a toll. I wanted to go away from that place and gather myself.

So that left three of us in a dilemma. I didn't know how to talk to Zahir. I looked at Vicky and he was no better. "Zahir, I have to leave now!" I said picking up my bag.

"Wait, I will drop you guys back!" Zahir said, as he drained the glass of beer.

It was half past ten and that left me with no choice other than joining him. So Vicky, Zahir and I went to the parking lot.

Since he was drunk, Vicky offered to drive the car and with a lot of reluctance, Zahir obliged. I sat back silently watching the night through the window. We humans can make anything possible; the night hardly seemed dark, looking at the golden rays coming from the street lights, radiating everywhere. But still nobody had found a solution to ward away the darkness present within them.

We have captured the sun, the wind, the water, but missed the vital thing called life! We try to rule others, put a condition, this is the way or that is the way. Who are we to decide that? Are we the creators? Do we have any power to lift a grain of sand without any assistance?

That night made me realize the important thing in life - love! It can be in any form but love by itself is pure and sacred.

My ocean of thoughts was put to an end by the four wheeled portable thing. The car screeched when Vicky applied the brakes, trying to avoid a truck. We had narrowly escaped an accident! Phew! Nothing happened.

I asked Vicky to be careful and he resumed driving. After a silent journey, I was dropped off to my place. Zahir was in deep sleep and I didn't bother disturbing him.

This was the most tiring day, but despite the heaviness, I couldn't sleep well. I was reminded of my cousin every second.

The next morning I had my bags packed and called up Zahir, "Hey listen, I have some important work. I won't be coming to the office for a few days!"

"Okay, no problem. Vicky and I will manage, but what important work do you have?" Zahir asked.

"I need to go to my native place. I will be back soon; bye, take care, and ya, please inform Mr.Ranganathan."

My train was scheduled to depart at 1:00 pm for my native place, Dharwad. I boarded the train on time. My parents stayed there along with my relatives. Dharwad is around an eight-hour journey from Bangalore. I reached there by 9.30 in the night. My brother, Datta, had come to the station to pick me up.

I reached home and met my parents and grandparents; it was a grand welcome. My favourite dishes were prepared, and the whole house was spic and span. They were very excited that their daughter was returning after one year. So after a lot of gossip and chit chatting, I was allowed to go to bed. It was 1 in the morning by the time I was actually sleeping.

"So when are you going to get married, my dear?" my granny asked me as she served hot *pakodas* the next evening.

"Oh granny, come on; I am too young for marriage," I said with disinterest.

"Twenty three is not young. I got married when I was just sixteen, you know," she said, as if marriage was a big achievement in one's life.

"Whatever granny; I am not ready for it..." Before I could continue further, she interrupted, "In my friend's neighbourhood, there is a guy; he is so handsome and earns well. He is settled in the US..."

"Granny please, I am still not ready for that," I said seriously.

"Okay dear, as you wish; who are we to advice these days? We are just your well wishers. You people are learned; you know the world better." She sighed and slowly walked towards the kitchen.

Oh god! Now these emotional blackmails; how I dread these things. But I had no choice; I had to listen to the lectures during my entire stay.

"Granny, please don't feel bad..." I went towards the kitchen to pacify my granny.

That night, my mother, my aunt, my granny and I, all of us were on the terrace, talking. I thought this was the best time to talk about my cousin and asked them.

"Granny, I remember there was an issue long ago

regarding Rashmi..." I had touched upon a sensitive issue and was ready to get backfired any moment.

"Don't talk about her my dear; my heart still cries whenever somebody mentions about that girl," granny said holding her hand near her bosom.

"I don't know why God becomes pitiless at times. Poor child, it shouldn't have happened," she continued. Now tears started trickling slowly down her wrinkled cheeks.

"Oh granny, please don't cry..." I said and wiped her tears. "Sorry, I won't raise this topic again," I said.

"No my dear, it's fine; granny gets emotional all the time," my aunt said.

"Go sleep now, it's getting late," my granny said and all of us returned to our rooms.

The next morning, I got up early and was ready.

"Oh, you are up already. And the new dress? Why are you wearing a new dress at home? First of all, you people spend a lot on these unwanted things. How much did this cost?" she asked as if I was wearing a Gucci gown or something.

"*Uff!* Oh granny, it's not very costly, don't worry. And I am planning to go to Kamala *masi's* house today. I haven't met her since the last two years," I said searching for the comb.

"Kamala's house? Why? What work do you have there?" She stood with her hands on her hips.

"Granny, you look like my hostel matron if you stand like this and ask questions," I said and started laughing.

"That is good; at least somebody like me is there to control you youngsters."

"Okay, I will tell you everything when I come back. Now I will leave. I asked Datta to drop me near his place." I took my bag and bid goodbye to everyone.

"Ask him to go slow on the bike; he drives as if he has to catch a train. That day I sat behind him with a bag full of vegetables and…"

"Okay granny, bye; he is getting late," I cut her short and rushed out.

"Careful…" my granny screamed from inside. I felt the whole world could have heard her.

"Koo, talk properly okay? They are already hurt, so don't bother them too much. A 'hi', 'hello', will do," my brother said as we reached my aunt's place.

"Okay, I'll be well behaved," I said and opened the gate. I rang the bell and waited for sometime.

"Wait, I am coming," I could hear my aunt's voice.

"Namaste Masi, how are you?" I greeted her folding my hands as soon as she opened the door.

"Oh my God! It's you! What a pleasant surprise. Come in, come in!" she said and hugged me.

They had shifted a long time back from Belgaum. Since my uncle was in politics, he would usually travel from place to place for some errands, so they decided to shift to Dharwad where they could rely on a few relatives if need be.

"Your uncle has gone to Rona (a place near Dharwad); some issues with farmers, and I am preparing batter to make *papad.*"

In the living room, there hung a picture of my cousin, smiling. I stood for some time staring at the picture. 'So pretty and innocent; no wonder Zahir fell for her.'

"So, what are you doing now? Still working in the same

company?" she asked.

"Yes Masi, I haven't changed my job," I said still looking at my cousin's photo.

"Last week I prepared *avalakki;* taste it. I know you like them," she said and laid a plate full of them in front of me.

She came out and saw that I was looking at the photo. "Your uncle likes this photo a lot."

"Uh… ya… she is looking very pretty in this."

"Life is not so good dear," she said wiping the photo. "It was not her mistake, but the age, spoilt her."

"Next month is her birthday; she would have turned 27!"

I wanted to console her but couldn't find words. My cousin Rashmi died of cancer three years back. It was a shock to all of us. Cancer at that young age was unheard of.

"Masi, it's okay; I am also your daughter am I not?"

Now the sobs turned into tears. She started crying. "We loved her so much. Why did god snatch her away from us?"

I immediately got up and held her. "*Masi,* come sit; please stop crying or else even I will start crying."

"Okay, sorry, I just remembered her when I saw you," she said wiping her tears.

"*Masi,* if you don't mind, can I ask something?"

She simply nodded. "*Masi,* did Rashmi discuss about her personal life with you?"

"No, initially when she was having an affair with that boy, she didn't say anything. But later on, she became very close, and during the time when she was getting treated for cancer, we bonded well. During that time she spoke about him."

"*Masi*, do you know about that guy?" I asked half expecting she would throw me out of the house.

"No, I don't intend to know."

After this, I didn't dare to talk about Rashmi. She was already upset and I didn't want to aggravate the pain.

"*Masi* I got something for you," I said and opened my bag and handed her a cover.

"What is this dear? At this age who wants gifts and all? Why did you spend so much for this old lady?"

"First open the gift and tell me how it is."

She tore open the wrapper. "Wah! What a nice sari, good selection." She opened the sari and started admiring it.

After a pause, she hugged me and said, "Thanks a lot dear; you are equal to my daughter. God bless you, dear."

"Now don't get emotional again. I have to rework on my make up." Both of us started laughing.

"Very tasty it is; can you pack some *avalakki?* I will take them to Bangalore," I said munching on a few.

"Why not? Wait, I will pack it neatly and give it to you."

We chatted happily for one hour. "*Masi*, I need to go now; mom and granny are waiting," I said looking at the old clock.

"Wait, I have to show you something," she said and went to the room.

"Here, take this." She handed me an old diary. "This is Rashmi's diary. I have preserved it for all these years; I couldn't read it myself nor give it."

"Then why are you giving it to me?" I asked her.

"I don't trust anyone that easily. I want to know what she has written in that; it's in English; I can barely read it. I cannot give this to her father or to my relatives. I want you to read it and tell me what my child thought."

"Okay, I will take this with me and give it back when I come here next time. Most probably I will be here for the next month's festival," I said and took leave.

I handled the diary with utmost care. I went home and dashed to my room.

"*Arre*, what happened?" my granny called after me.

"Nothing, I will come back and tell you," I said and locked my room.

I sat on the bed and carefully opened the diary.

'My best friend' was written in bold. Though the letters were faded, it gave an impression of it being colourfully done once upon a time.

The first few pages were a random scribble about her school friends, the gossip and daily routines. I ran through them not giving them much importance. Then my eyes stopped at one page.

I joined an engineering college…. I knew I was on the right track. I read with utmost interest.

"What are you doing inside for such a long time?" My granny knocked my room door with such force that even a dead person would come out alive.

"Coming," I said and hurriedly closed the diary and kept it in my bag.

"What is it granny?" I grumbled as I opened the door.

"It's almost dinner time dear. Why don't you eat something?" She caringly caressed my head. "Why do you look so stressed? Did something happen in

Kamala's house?"

"No granny, we just discussed a few things here and there. Of course Masi cried when Rashmi's topic came up. But she became normal after sometime," I said.

"Okay, now come for dinner. I have prepared your favourite food," she said half dragging me towards the kitchen.

At night, when everyone went off to sleep, I got up and searched for the diary in my bag. Since there was no bed lamp, I decided to sit in the living room.

I read carefully page by page. Then after about some twenty pages, she had mentioned about Zahir. From her extracts, it appeared that she too was drawn towards him even before there was a formal proposal.

She had mentioned in detail how she felt when he would constantly stare at her. The description was so well written that I felt like I was actually watching a movie. Some of the entries were, *'Today, I wore a peacock blue salwar with a very mild handwork near the neck. Now why do you think I am mentioning this? Because the truth that I was seeking all these days surfaced today.*

He had never seen me in this dress; I was wearing it for the first time and was anticipating his reaction. I stepped out of the bus and scanned the college arena for his glance. But he was nowhere in sight. Even though I received many compliments, the icing on the cake was still missing. I went to the class but still couldn't find him. After about an hour, I got to know that he had to go to some debate competition. I felt so bad, I don't know why. I mean, he wasn't my best friend or something. We used to casually chat about college stuff once in a while, but still I was strongly drawn towards him. So dejected, I sat through the classes. It was evening, around four, and everyone crowded near the bus stop. I too went there along with my friends. Suddenly I heard someone call me from behind and to my great surprise, I saw him! He was standing there sheepishly. I excused myself from my friends and went to him; I could feel his eyes perched on me like a radar tracking the signal. I smiled to myself and said 'hi' to him. He too smiled and said a feeble 'hi'. I had never seen him being so nervous. He said he wanted some notes and asked whether I could lend my book. Though I had told my friend that I would be giving it to her, I promptly gave the book to him.

He asked me if my salwar was new, then fumbled and said that I was looking good. I was waiting for this moment since morning. He tried to say something but stopped. 'Maybe later,' he said and went away.

I joined my friends who were now pulling my leg. From a common friend I came to know that he had already borrowed the books from his friend and nobody knew why exactly he had come back to college.

I don't know about others, but I feel when you are attracted to someone, their one glance means a lot; their one word, one smile, can give you so much joy and fill your heart with some unknown feeling. Today I too felt the same. I was constantly thinking about him and in fact, I turned back to see if he was there. There he was, standing with his friends but still looking in my direction, and when our eyes met, I turned away from him. Throughout the journey I silently sat near the window. Is it love? Maybe or maybe not. But there is something in that glance; when he looks deep into my eyes, I feel a shudder deep down. The whole world comes to a sudden standstill and I feel there is no one around except us.

What is happening to me? I should stop all this immediately. He is just a friend and I should not encourage this. Now it's time for me to sleep…'

I looked at the clock; it was 2 in the morning, so forcibly I replaced her diary and went to sleep. But I was very restless. I wanted to know the reason why she said 'no' to Zahir. From whatever she had written about him, I could make out that she was in love with him right from the beginning. With so much running in my mind, I went off to sleep hoping to find out the truth the next day.

The next day, I got up at 8 in the morning and could see no one around. Some noises were coming from the kitchen and my granny was super active as usual.

"Granny, what are you doing and why is everyone busy today?" I asked hugging her.

"Dirty girl; you have just got up. I have already finished my bath. Go, at least brush your teeth," she said.

"Okay I will go but first tell me what you people are doing."

"You have to go back tonight to Bangalore, if you remember."

"Oh I forgot completely. I thought it was tomorrow. Okay I will go and pack my bag, and please granny, don't give me a truck load of things to eat. First of all, people say I look so full and filled!" I said walking towards the wash room.

"That's how Indian women are meant to be," she said and started laughing. I could hear my aunt and mom too join her.

It was time to leave. I got my luggage and bade farewell to them. My granny was as usual in tears; my mom and aunt too started to cry. I told them that I would come again next month which resulted in putting smiles on their faces. It was difficult for me too; I too was in tears but controlled them. Finally I was dropped off to the railway station and my bossy brother did some final advising - don't go here, don't talk, blah blah. I just nodded my head agreeing with everything and sat in my berth.

As the train picked up speed, I looked around my boogie. A couple had occupied the upper berth and two middle aged women and I, were seated in the lower berth. They tried to strike a conversation with me but I didn't bother much and pretended to be busy staring at the night outside.

I reached Bangalore in the early morning, took an auto to my room and before I could even unpack, I opened her diary to finish reading the remaining pages.

It was really touching to know how she had felt for him. Her feelings were so true and pure. Then came the most awaited event; I was shocked to read it. I just couldn't hold back my tears. I felt so very bad for her and blamed god for all this.

She had mentioned clearly why she left Zahir, or why she said 'no' to Zahir. For a second, I got angry with Zahir for not understanding her. I almost called Zahir to tell him about this but held back thinking there would be the right moment and right time to do all this.

The sacrifice, the love, the pain she underwent could not be justified by words. Zahir knew nothing about her death and that pained me, but it was the past and nothing could be done now. My only concern was the hatred that Zahir carried with him which came in his path of becoming a better person. If that had to be removed, recalling his past was a must. So I decided to talk to Zahir regarding this as early as possible. I would be going back to office the next day so I thought I would sort it out with him and relieve him of the burden that he carried all these years.

I thought love can overpower anything, but was wrong!

CHAPTER 12
THE BEGINNING

"I am going to Paris," Zahir said waving his hand, as soon as I came to office.

"What's the reason? You won a lottery or your mother-in-law is sponsoring it?" I asked pulling my chair.

"You remember we had quoted for that high profile project for a power plant in France?"

"Oh that one, which we quoted almost a year back…"

"Exactly, it's the finalization meeting."

"So the marketing guys must be going."

"No, it's a technical meeting and Doctor wants me to go for the meeting."

"Oh, that's good," I said. I was thinking about how to start the conversation about Rashmi.

"What happened? Something bothering you?" he asked.

"What about me going to Paris?"

"He has not said anything about you."

"Yaar, I want to got to that place, it is heaven."

"You will definitely get more chances in future; stay focused," Zahir said.

"Okay," I said and started working with a dejected face.

He was busy preparing for the meeting abroad so I didn't get a chance to talk about her.

Two days later…

The phone rang.

I picked up the call. "Hello, Okay… ya… no problems."

I started jumping in joy. "Do you guys know who called?"

"No, was it your future husband?" Vicky asked.

"Shut up yaar, it was Doctor's secretary.

"So what? She calls Zahir all the time; what's new?" Vicky again asked.

"I am going to Paris," I said and enacted a ballet.

"Oh hello madam, everything okay?"Vicky asked looking strangely at me.

"Yuppie I am so happy," I said turning around trying to balance on my toes.

"I hope you don't end up in hospital with a broken leg," Zahir said and pulled me back to my seat.

Later, I came to know that Zahir had recommended my name and he had fought with Doctor to take me because of my dedication to that project and knowledge about that project. Doctor had finally agreed. The trip was scheduled after a fortnight. All the formalities of the Schengen visa and all other travel requirements like insurance were completed in ten days and we were on board Air France.

"Hey, have you packed warm clothing? It's cold there," Zahir said.

"Yeah, don't worry; I am used to it," I said smiling.

"What bloody used to it, it's two degrees. You will freeze to death with the kind of clothes you are wearing," Doctor interrupted.

"Yeah Doctor, I have brought warm clothing and packed some ready-to-eat meals," I said

I told Zahir that I had not got any warm clothes. He told me not to worry and gave me one of his extra jackets.

We reached at 7 in the morning and came out of the Charles De Gaul airport. I felt as if I was stepping into a refrigerator. It was the first time I experienced such extreme weather.

"Call the taxi; we have to go to the hotel," Doctor said pushing his stroller.

"Sir, it's coming; we will board this one," Zahir said.

"What's the name of the hotel? I forgot," I whispered to Zahir.

"Hotel Paul rive Gauche Elysees Paris."

"No wonder I couldn't get the name. Phew! By the time I learn the hotel's name, we would have finished our seminar," I giggled as I pushed my stroller.

Zahir smiled and asked me to hurry to keep pace with Doctor.

We boarded the taxi. It was a GPS navigated taxi and there was absolutely no problem finding the hotel. I was awestruck at the development in Europe. I am sure our country needs another decade to have this kind of system.

"Get ready by eleven; we have to go for a meeting," Doctor said before going to his room in the hotel.

"Sir, but we have the meeting tomorrow," I said.

"Your highness, we have not come for a picnic," Doctor remarked and I had to just shut my mouth.

"Just keep quiet; don't talk too much in front of him," Zahir said as we made our way to our rooms.

The rooms were lovely. My room was completely

white - white cushions, sofas, bed and even the walls. The room had a small balcony overlooking a terrace garden below. The wind pushed the white silk curtains as I opened the window. It was a very well maintained hotel. After carefully studying everything in the room (including the switches), I finally decided to freshen up.

I got a call from Zahir asking me to be ready in an hour. I ransacked my suitcase looking for the right dress to wear for the meeting. I finally decided on some chic office trousers.

We met Doctor at the hotel lobby and went to have breakfast. We had to survive on breads and butter. Zahir signalled to me not to grumble too much about food. So I was careful not to mention this topic in front of Doctor.

The meeting was held in an office which was an hour's drive from our hotel.

"Have you brought all the files?" Doctor enquired as we went to the meeting hall.

"Yes sir, we have got all the required files and we are ready," Zahir said.

The meeting was with an Indian marketing consultant who discussed about the bid happening tomorrow for the project.

After discussing for an hour, we shot off to the railway station. Doctor suggested we take a tube (train). He sat five seats away from us for God knows what reason. Zahir and I sat facing each other since both of us wanted window seats.

"Caught you," I said looking at Zahir.

"Caught what?"

"I know what you were looking at." I pointed to an attractive French blonde reading a fashion magazine sitting beside me wearing a skirt.

"No, I was just looking at the fashion magazine."

"Come on, I know which magazine you were looking at," I teased.

"Okay I give up, now leave me alone," Zahir said smiling and turned towards the window.

I continued troubling him during the entire journey. He listened to me patiently not showing any signs of anger.

We parted in the hotel to go to our rooms.

"Okay be prepared for the big day; it's a take or break situation," Doctor said.

"This is the only thing he says - be prepared, do this. Huh, can't he ever talk like normal beings?" I muttered to Zahir as Doctor closed his door.

"Forget that; we have to prepare a lot for tomorrow's meeting so be ready with everything," Zahir said.

At about 8 in the evening, we came down to have dinner but Doctor preferred to remain in his room. So Zahir and I discussed about tomorrow's meeting and went back to our rooms.

The next morning, Doctor was ready with his papers and files. He was always ahead of us in everything.

"We will have the meeting in one hour. Emphasize more on the technical issues so that they should know our competence. This contract is being bid by the world's best and we are a small company. We can compete with them only if we can show that we are determined,"

Doctor said before the meeting started.

"Okay Doctor; I am ready for the show," Zahir said.

"Khushi, you have to help him with the presentation; you are aware of all the intricacies of the project."

"Okay Doctor; I have prepared myself thoroughly."

The taxi was waiting for us at the hotel parking lot. We drove down and reached within half an hour.

"Bon jour," one of the French executives greeted us.

"Hi," Doctor shook his hand. We bowed down, shook hands with that French executive and went inside.

There was a group of very experienced people sitting in the room. There were four French engineers and one Indian engineer.

"Welcome," they greeted us and we had to start the presentation in the next five minutes.

"So let's start; you have only half an hour," one of the senior most French guys said sitting with his legs crossed.

Zahir had prepared the presentation. He started off in high spirits. The flow was good but he did not stress too much on the details. He skimmed through the process.

"Excuse me Mr. Zahir, could you please run the previous slide?" one of the technical French guys requested.

"Yes sir, sure," he said and clicked on the previous slide.

"Can you please explain this technology?" he asked.

"Sir… this is a rare technology that helps in capturing maximum available raw material…" Zahir fumbled a lot while explaining this.

"If I may correct you, this is not the technology we are looking for, "one of the French guys interrupted.

"Sir, you mentioned about green technology and what

we are proposing to you right now is considered one among the best," Zahir replied.

"Pardon me, but I don't seem to follow your presentation." The other French guy was furious. "Don't you understand that this is not the technology we are looking for? We had clearly written this in our specification."

"Sir, but this is the technology that is being used world wide."

"Our raw material does not support this technology. Have you gone through the specifications that we had given?"

We had done everything and we missed the most important part of the project.

"Did you go through the specifications clearly?" Doctor asked.

"Yes Doctor, I have been reading it."

"Have you analysed whether this fits into this technology?"

"Ah…" Zahir's head was down with shame.

"My sincere apologies for this mistake," Doctor apologized in front of the audience.

"Sir, please give us another chance," I asked them but they said they had to think about it.

We wound up and left. I was wondering how could Zahir miss such a vital thing. I wanted to ask him but Doctor was with us, so I remained quiet.

Silence prevailed in the cab. No one spoke, and Doctor was busy looking at the specifications. Zahir looked completely lost. Again my chance of talking to Zahir about Rashmi seemed dim. I had planned to speak to him on that day, but the situation was so tense and grim that I didn't want to start any new tension.

Doctor called us to his room as soon as we reached the hotel. We went to our rooms, freshened up and gathered in Doctor's room.

He stood near the balcony with hands behind him.

He had kept an old letter on the table; he asked us to read it. I took the sheet and we began reading.

"Aloud," he said.

"Dear Doctor," I started.

"Including the date," he said still not looking in our direction.

"Date March 9th 1970, Monday," I read.

"Dear Doctor,

I feel so proud to call you Doctor. First of all, congrats for proving me wrong. I remember the day when I removed you from my team when doing your PhD. I did not encourage you when you wanted to try something new. I always found you arrogant and not adhering to rules; this used to irk me. And do you remember the goof up that you had done? Your experiment failed miserably despite me telling you not to proceed with that.

I felt that humiliation would pull you back and you wouldn't be able to do anything. The struggle you made to get back in the driver's seat is commendable.

The university did not support you and you had to search for a new guide who had no clue about your work. You overcame all the debacles and grew to be one of the best in this field. I felt bad for you, was infuriated with your behaviour.

Now I honestly feel flawed in estimating you and your potential. I am writing this letter of appreciation not for your achievements, but for the way you regained from the fall. In my career of 35 years, I have seen many people fail but nobody emerged like you.

Hats off to you my boy! You will reach great heights .My blessings and support will be there with you till I breathe my last.

Your well wisher,

Dr. Derrick Cart

Director of University of Hunsman

I looked at Zahir when I finished reading. He was looking down. Then I turned towards Doctor. He too was looking away. Well, what was I supposed to do I don't know. So I carefully folded the letter and put it back on his table.

"Everyone does make mistakes; no one is perfect. But we can strive to achieve perfection," he said turning to us. "Today it was a great opportunity for both of you to showcase your talent, but it toppled. But never mind; as they say, failure is a stepping stone to success. I want you both to mend the situation by yourselves. I don't want to guide your every thought or action."

After a pause he added, "And remember, I myself have failed in life, but I never accepted defeat till the last moment, and I never will!"

We said we would give our hundred percent to this project and left for our rooms. On the way I said, "Now I feel much better after talking to Doctor. I was so worried about the consequences of the meeting," I said.

"Hmmm true; even I was sort of troubled regarding this," he said.

"But Zahir I feel there is something else too. You didn't

seem that fine since yesterday. Very silent and looking a bit disturbed."

"*Nahi yaar*, I am concerned about the project."

"No boss, there is something else written on your face."

"Khushi, can you leave me alone for sometime?"

"Yes I will! Is it someone's birthday today?" I asked.

"What have I got to do with someone's birthday?" he said irately.

"Okay, I know today is Rashmi's birthday!"

"Who Rashmi? I don't know anyone by that name," he said.

"Zahir let's take a walk. I need to talk to you about something important," I nudged him.

"No I am not in any mood for a jolly ride. Let's get back to our rooms. Tomorrow is a big day, and I hope you know that!"

"It's about Rashmi!" I said unsmiling.

"I don't want to talk about her!" he said sternly.

"But I want to and I am not taking 'no' for an answer."

"Okay fine, say," he said as we went to the front lounge in the hotel. We sat on a lofty chair over which was lit a dazzling chandelier made of diamond shaped crystals. It gave a very elegant look, but no amount of exterior bliss helped us to uplift our dead spirits.

The lights were more disturbing than comforting, so we went out in the gardens. A moonless cold night it was, but we preferred that place since it had a very beautiful garden surrounded by well maintained shrubs.

"Yeah it's her birthday. I am disturbed since morning. I am sorry for my boorish behaviour," he said looking up at the sky.

"I knew about it. But don't you think it's high time you let go of the past?" I said.

"I would have if I knew the reason why she ditched me. If it is a genuine reason, then why did she hide it from me? Why punish me for nothing? I am carrying this load since the last six years. You may say it's a long time, but a four-year love cannot get over in a few years. It's like you cannot hate it nor can you love. You think I have not tried to come out of it? I have, in every possible way, but only one snag remains; why did she leave me? I wanted to talk to her; I even tried calling her but she wouldn't answer. I waited, but it still didn't get any results, so after a year, I went to Mumbai.

I was happy that he was finally talking about his past. It seemed like a worm breaking its cocoon desperately seeking the world outside. I remained quiet and allowed him to speak.

He continued, "Mumbai is so diversified. The experiences there made me forget about her though not completely. It covered the wound for the time being. I worked there for a year and 3 months, got bored of *Vada-pavs, chowpathi,* and the hustle-bustle life. I planned to go to Bangalore and got myself another decent job, but I had changed myself completely. I was never this serious; my mantra in life was 'ke sera sera', whatever will be, will be. My life was going in a perfect way, everything happened as desired. But my dreams were shattered. I lost the zeal, I lost myself. I wanted to be a loner and lead my life aloof. When I was talking to you, I was forced to get back into my old form, but that too couldn't stay for long.

Just when I thought I was becoming better, my old friend Roopak came in. Again I was pulled into my past. Today is her birthday; I just cannot forget her."

"Zahir, Rashmi was my cousin!" I said looking at him.

"What?" he said getting up, "I don't believe you."

"Yes, it's true. I came to know when Roopak told us your story. I too was shocked at first and was not convinced till I went to my native place to make enquiries."

"What are you saying?" Zahir was still unconvinced.

"She was my distant cousin. I was very close to her during our childhood, but the distance grew because I came to Bangalore to study and she went to Belgaum."

"Zahir…" I paused a bit not sure how to continue.

"What?" he asked.

"Rashmi is… no more!"

Zahir froze there, he stood still. It was a big shock to him. "What the hell are you saying?"

"Calm down, please. Rashmi was diagnosed with cancer. Doctors told her she won't live more than a year."

"No, this is not true. She was very healthy. I have never seen her ill or she would have told me."

"Even she did not know about her illness; she came to know very late. It was at a critical stage. She ignored all the minor hints that showed up during her illness and this ignorance led to her death." By now I was unable to hold back my tears and burst out.

"When did she die?" he asked.

"She died on 3rd Feb. I am sorry I couldn't tell you before. I…have her diary with me."

"Why did she not tell me about this?"

"Do I still have to tell you? It is clear she wanted you to stay happy. She knew that you loved her a lot and this news would destroy you completely and she even spoke to your friends regarding this and asked them to talk you out of this relation."

He held back his tears. I could see him struggle. "This is too unreal. I cannot believe it."

"All of them were loyal to you. Whatever sacrifices they made was to keep you happy. I think it's better you read the diary and find out for yourself," I said.

There was no reaction from him; he was cold and speechless. He fell down on his knees and started crying. "Zahir, please don't cry…" No matter what I said, the tears did not stop.

"How could I? How could I do this? Why did I not trust her? I want her back… I cannot stay without her. I want to die. I suspected my friends, my good friends. What was wrong with me?" Zahir was like a kid crying uncontrollably. It was very difficult to see him in that state. I thought it best to leave him alone for some time and so I left.

There was a soft knock on my door; I opened it to find Zahir standing there. I called him inside; he walked like a dead soul and slumped on the chair.

"Khushi, can you give me her diary?" he asked.

"Yes, I will give it with only one condition that no matter what you feel now, tomorrow we have to give our best."

"I don't know anything now. What is the use of my life?"

"That is precisely why I never felt like showing the

diary to you all these days. Rashmi always wanted you to be happy in life and even though she was tempted to talk to you, she did not lose her self control, not to see you suffer like this."

"What am I going to achieve? For whose sake?"

"For Rashmi's sake!"I retorted. "She didn't want to be the reason for your failure in life and if you behave like this, I don't think she would be happy."

He sat there lost in thought, his mind was blown into pieces. He wanted to cry, wanted to run away; there was a surge of emotions. I watched him struggle helplessly. I went up to him and opened the last sheet of the diary in which Rashmi had poured her heart out.

'Zahir means so much to me. I cannot see him hurt. Forgive me if I hurt him and whatever I am doing is for his sake. If I tell him about my disease, he will become weak. Please give me the strength to carry on with my lie. Tomorrow is the last day in my life that I will meet him. Give me strength to withstand his pain, his confusion and his anger. I wish he becomes successful in life and stays happy wherever he is. I don't mind his resentment towards me, but I cannot bear to see him lose the thing for life. Today I met his friends; with all my pleas they have agreed to talk as per my instruction. I could see Roopak in tears, and he was torn between his grief for me and his best friend. I just hope everything goes as planned.'

"I hope this will give you some inspiration," I said closing the diary. "You have to perform very well tomorrow. If we bag this project, then chances of getting a promotion are high; more than that, you will have job satisfaction."

"Hmmm," he said.

"Think about it; pain is inevitable, nobody can stop it, but controlling it is in your hands, "I said convincingly.

"I have decided not to give you the diary till you finish your presentation."

"Okay, I better go to my room; it's pretty late. Be prepared for tomorrow; don't count on me."

"But..."

"Good night," he said closing the door behind him.

I was flipping through the documents for the hundredth time, when sitting in the meeting room. Doctor was busy talking to some other members while I was constantly looking at the time and wondering why the hell Zahir had not come. The presentation was fixed at 11 in the morning and it was fifteen minutes more to go. I sat there looking at the door then shifting my glance towards the clock. Then at sharp eleven, everyone came in except for the man in need.

Doctor looked at me indicating that I start the presentation. I took the cue, adjusted the laptop and started the presentation. "Excuse me." Someone knocked on the door and entered; it was one of the office boys. He politely gave the cordless phone to Doctor.

Doctor got up and excused himself. He came in after five minutes and said, "Gentlemen, let's take a small break for fifteen minutes. We have a very elite person joining us. I apologize for this inconvenience." Everyone agreed and went out for an early tea break.

"Doctor, who was it?" I asked curiously.

"Zahir called; he is bringing some person with him. Let's see how beneficial he can be for us."

"Hope so," I said and drowned into my laptop wondering what Zahir was up to.

After fifteen minutes, everyone again joined in. There was still no sign of Zahir. Doctor asked me to call Zahir. Since it was getting late, another bidder from Netherlands started his presentation. I tried calling him but there was no reply. Then I saw two people emerge out of the lift - one was Zahir and the other was an elegant man, with a warm smile on his face.

Before anyone could speak, I rushed inside the room and told Doctor that he had arrived with that person.

"Sorry to keep you waiting, but this was really required for the meeting." Zahir apologized to the people present. "I would like to introduce this gentleman from Green Tech, Munich - Dr. Rudolf Adler."

"Hello," he said heartily; the entire crowd stood up in astonishment.

"Gosh, Dr Rudolf, we are extremely pleased to meet you," one person greeted him enthusiastically.

"It's overwhelming; oh gosh, great to see you here amongst us Dr Rudolf," said another.

I was bewildered and just out of curiosity, googled his name only to find that he was the CEO of the most sort out company in this technology and he was one of the 'who's who' in this field . I was shocked; how on earth did Zahir manage to rope him here?

"Okay guys, thanks a lot. It's a pleasure meeting you all. Let me tell you how I landed up here. This guy," he said pointing at Zahir, "is dynamite. He called me last night and said, 'Your technology is substandard; who in this world will like to have their engines run by apricots and nuts scrap. I bet your power supply-demand is always at stake looking at the kind of raw material you use.' I wanted to cut the call and go back to sleep but no, this guy did not give up till I got irritated and pulled out a few of my hair. I wanted to meet him in person and decided to take him to a site where it was in steady condition. When I met him, he said there were a bunch of others that were in the same condition and asked me whether I could take them all. That brought me here," he said smiling pleasantly.

Zahir had a spark in his eyes; I felt the old Zahir was back. Now the presentation was a cake walk. Doctor Rudolf was our trump card; he was a pioneer in the technology that we had suggested. It turned out that the customers were so thrilled that before the conclusion of the meeting, they gave us a date for their final meeting. "We really appreciate your generosity. In spite of your hectic schedule, you took time for us; we shall remain in dept for your thoughtfulness," Doctor exclaimed to Doctor Rudolf.

"Oh, it's my pleasure. It was the technology and the scepticism amongst the people that drew me here. We need to build green and clean technologies for the future; some sort of contribution back to nature. And all because of your boy here, the sly fox, I came here," he said patting Zahir.

After exchanging pleasantries, we left. Doctor escorted him till his car. "Yuppie..." I jumped and threw my arms around Zahir.

"You are awesome. I am so happy," I said super excitedly.

"Nothing *yaar*, last night I was searching for the supports for such new technology and found his company. I had a tough time convincing his secretary for his phone number, but I did not realize it could have such a massive impact. I started with an idea and it clicked for us." He beamed.

"Oh Zahir, wonderful," I exclaimed again.

"I did this for Rashmi; she took the risk, she put up an act even though she knew I would hate her for all those things, she took the blame on her so casually as if she really was not interested in me and all this was just to make me successful in life. Nothing mattered to her other than my happiness. And such sacrifices should not go in vain. This is my way of telling her thanks, that's it," he said smiling.

"I know ..." I said with tears in my eyes.

As we moved along the long corridor, he turned towards me and said, "I have to give credit to someone too." He looked straight at me and began with a serious note, "I dedicate this to my love Rashmi and to some fatso," he burst out laughing.

"What? Come again? What do you mean?"I said and started running behind him.

"Ha ha ha..."

EPILOGUE

The characters (especially friends of Zahir) involved are very much alive and are thanking their stars that their real names are not brought to light. We wanted to put their photos too just to bring life to the characters and unfortunately, couldn't go ahead as planned. If they get a chance to meet either of us (which seems distant because they are settled in far off lands) all hell is going to break loose. This book is dedicated to them and to our friendship which we cherish to this day and in a way, this is our thanks to them for being there only through good times and abandoning us when things went wrong.

-- The End --

Acknowledgement

Two days and a half, we are still making a list of all those we need to thank. But, it's worth all the time. Without the support of these people, we would have never seen our names printed on a book.

I (Trupthi) should actually thank my friend-cum-co-author-cum-colleague (Zeeshan) for making it possible; I thank him for the patience he had, to notice the nitty gritties while reviewing my bit of work. I thank him for the patience he had while I argued relentlessly convincing him and did not budge to change or rectify my mistakes.

I thank my husband (Narayan) and my in-laws, who supported me in every way they could and put up with my "I-AM-AN–AUTHOR-NOW "attitude even before I actually penned down a few pages. (Though am angry with him falling off his seat the minute I mentioned about the book!)

I thank Issy Jacob, my dear friend, for believing that I could pen down my feelings better than designing heat exchangers. I thank my notorious class of M.S. Ramaiah Institute of Technology, Bangalore, for being a source for this book. (I would love to see their smiles after reading this!)

I thank my parents for rendering their support. And I thank my sister for giving me honest feedback whenever not required.

I thank the coincidence that brought Zeeshan back into the organization (where we are currently working), which he had left earlier in search of better prospects.

I thank his friends (Praveen Ghorpade, Deepak Khyadi, Mubbashir Jamadar, Suhas Shastry, Aftab Ali Bankapure and Praveen Kumar Singh), from KLE College of Engineering and Technology, Belgaum, for being the real source of inspiration for us to write this book.

I thank his wife (Shameem), for being tolerant with him, even though he would end up romancing the manuscripts night after night. Her moral support in all ways was a big boost.

We would like to thank the editorial team and especially late Mr. Sunil Poolani from Leadstart for giving us a chance to bring out this book.

We would like to thank our God Almighty for giving us support when we needed it the most.

With lots of love,

From Trups and Zee